SOCIETY OF BIBLICAL LITERATURE

DISSERTATION SERIES

edited by

Howard C. Kee

and

Douglas A. Knight

Number 21

STUDIES IN ANCIENT YAHWISTIC POETRY

by

Frank Moore Cross, Jr.

David Noel Freedman

SCHOLARS PRESS
Missoula, Montana

STUDIES IN ANCIENT YAHWISTIC POETRY

by

Frank Moore Cross, Jr.

David Noel Freedman

Published by

SCHOLARS PRESS

for

The Society of Biblical Literature

Distributed by

SCHOLARS PRESS
University of Montana
Missoula, Montana 59801

STUDIES IN ANCIENT YAHWISTIC POETRY

by

Frank Moore Cross, Jr.

David Noel Freedman

Frank Moore Cross, Jr.
Ph.D., 1950
Johns Hopkins University

Advisor:
W. F. Albright

David Noel Freedman
Ph.D., 1948
Johns Hopkins University

Advisor:
W. F. Albright

Library of Congress Cataloging in Publication Data

Cross, Frank Moore.
Studies in ancient Yahwistic poetry.

(SBL dissertation series)
Bibliography: p.
1. Hebrew poetry, Biblical--History and criticism.
2. Bible. O.T. Exodus XV--Criticism, Textual.
3. Bible. OT. Genesis XLIX--Criticism, Textual.
4. Bible. O.T. Deuteronomy XXXIII--Criticism,
Textual. 5. Bible. O.T. 2 Samuel XXII--Criticism,
Textual. 6. Bible. O.T. Psalms XVIII--Criticism,
Textual. I. Freedman, David Noel, 1922- joint
author. II. Title. III. Series: Society of
Biblical Literature. Dissertation series.

BS1405.2.C76 222 75-28159
ISBN 0-89130-014-7

Printed in the United States of America
1 2 3 4 5
Printing Department
University of Montana
Missoula, Montana 59801

PREFACE

This study is the second of two joint doctoral dissertations submitted to the Board of University Studies of the Johns Hopkins University by David Noel Freedman and Frank Moore Cross.

The first: The Evolution of Early Hebrew Orthography: The Epigraphic Evidence was submitted in 1948.

The second: Studies in Ancient Yahwistic Poetry was submitted in 1950.

The second dissertation is here reproduced without change--except for the correction of typographic errors and normalization of abbreviations and bibliographical references. A *Postscriptum* is added to the dissertation, written twenty-five years after the dissertation was submitted, to give our present perspective upon our early work.

TABLE OF CONTENTS

CHAPTER I

INTRODUCTION TO THE STUDIES

CHAPTER I

INTRODUCTION TO THE STUDIES

Ancient Yahwistic poetry is a peculiarly tempting field of study. In this small body of literature are preserved the oldest expressions of Israel's faith. It reveals a conception of God at once intuitive and concrete, born of vividly direct experience and participation in his mighty acts, a conception devoid of the sophistication and formalism which result from centuries of theological speculation. The language of the poems is rich and exuberant, the imagery is picturesque, the figures of speech extravagant. The compositions are marked by a strong rhythm, with a regular musical beat, frequently organized into strophes of considerable complexity. Altogether, they are the product of the most dynamic and creative era of Israel's literary enterprise.

Scholarly interest and research in this poetry have always been extensive, owing to the antiquity and significance of the material. Besides, the serious textual difficulties (the by-product of centuries of oral and written transmission) and linguistic obscurities have been a challenge to students for many generations.

Aside from the perennial attraction of this corpus of ancient poetry for the scholar, there are compelling reasons for fresh investigation at the present time. Archaeological research has supplied, in recent years, a large collection of literary materials bearing upon old Israelite poetry. The intensive study of this material, its content, form and style, its paleography and orthography, has resulted in the development of radically new and scientifically tested procedures, directly applicable to the biblical corpus.

The older scholarship was limited by the paucity of extra-biblical materials. It was concentrated largely upon the Hebrew text and versions, with occasional reference to surviving monuments of antiquity, and information preserved in classical sources. The results too frequently were without solid foundation, though many brilliant conjectures have since been confirmed by newer evidence. Investigation was circumscribed further by the general adherence to a rigidly conceived reconstruction of the evolution of Hebrew thought and history. The dogmas of a nineteenth century *Weltanschauung*, especially those based upon the dialectics of German idealism, took the place of scientific caution in dealing with matters where factual evidence was largely lacking.

In the case of Old Testament poetry, date of composition and determination of the immediate historical circumstances were chief goals of scholarly interest. The poems were dissected, each fragment being identified by its presumed conceptual outlook and then assigned to the corresponding period in the artificially reconstructed history of Hebrew thought and religion. In addition, obscure allusions were extracted from the poems, and correlated with almost equally obscure events and persons in determining the historical occasion of the segments. The historical study of the grammar and vocabulary had not yet progressed sufficiently to be of help in the analysis or dating of a poem. Similarly there were too few examples of contemporary Near Eastern poetry to be used in the classification of biblical types and forms.

Today, as a result of the remarkable progress of scientific research and synthesis, stemming from the archaeological excavations of innumerable sites in the Near East, our understanding of the history of Israel and the development of the Old Testament faith has been transformed. Israel has been placed in her ancient setting, the social and cultural environment, the conceptual world. There is now an extraordinary amount of linguistic material relating to the study of Hebrew. A profusion of literary texts has come to light, which provide an ample basis for the comparative study of Old Testament literature. Thus new scientific controls are added to the fundamental principles of historical and textual criticism of past generations. New hypotheses, reconstructions, and syntheses taking into account the new data, may now replace the limited and subjective speculations of former times. In no area of Old Testament study are these developments better applicable than in the analysis of early Yahwistic poetry.

There are, in particular, two new techniques available for the reexamination of early Hebrew poetry. The first, detailed *orthographic analysis*, is based upon our present understanding of the evolution of early Hebrew orthography. This was made possible by the accurate dating and effective interpretation of the early Phoenician, Aramaic, and Hebrew inscriptions. The epigraphic evidence was sufficiently sifted in 1944 to permit W. F. Albright's reconstruction of the Oracles of Balaam in the older orthography.[1] This treatment fixed a date in the tenth century for the written composition of the Oracles, and also provided important insights into hitherto unnoticed sources of corruption and misinterpretation of the text.

The other technique, specialized *linguistic analysis*, derives from the study and decipherment of the Canaanite cuneiform texts from Ras Shamrah, their linguistic structure and vocabulary, their poetic style and metrical forms. The application of this knowledge to biblical poetry is perhaps the most significant factor in the new studies.[2]

The corpus of ancient Yahwistic poetry has not yet been delineated in satisfactory fashion. The proper starting point is the Song of Deborah, a victory hymn, the occasion of which is known, and the approximate date quite certain, i.e., ca. 1100 B.C. Burney's study of this poem[3] is of basic importance; he described the phenomenon of climactic parallelism, a characteristic feature of the Song of Deborah, and now very familiar from the Ugaritic epics. Albright, in a subsequent treatment[4], went further in the analysis of the metrical and strophic pattern of the poem, and also set it in the context of the comparative materials available from Mesopotamia and Egypt. The present partial study follows the lines laid out in these treatments.[5] This victory hymn, one of the oldest and most dramatic specimens of early Yahwistic poetry, belongs to the same general period as the other great victory songs so far known from the ancient world: the hymn of Rameses II after the battle with the Hittites at Kadesh, the poems describing the victory of Merneptah over the Libyans, and Rameses III over the Sea Peoples, and the victory hymn of Tukulti-Ninurta I, after his defeat of the Cossaeans. The Song of Deborah is also to be grouped with the Song of Miriam (Ex. 15) celebrating the destruction of Pharaoh's host in the Reed Sea.[6]

Though this was not generally recognized by the older scholars, it is clear that the victory hymn in Exodus 15 is a literary unit.[7] It has the same antiphonal character and metrical form as the Song of Deborah. Its linguistic features are genuinely archaic, contrary to the standard view that they show late Aramaic influence and are otherwise pseudo-archaic. Orthographic evidence supports a tenth-century date as the latest for the written text of the poem. Historical analysis of the text shows that the hymn is our earliest and most reliable source for reconstructing the actual sequence of events in the passage of the Reed Sea.[8] This confirms the conclusions drawn from the literary, linguistic, and orthographic examination of the song.

The Oracles of Balaam belong to the category of oracles delivered by a seer before battle. It is the finest early example of this type, which is closely associated with the victory hymn. Albright's treatment of the Balaam series has antiquated all previous studies not only of this poem but of the other poems in the corpus. His masterful use of old and new disciplines makes the short study an indispensable preparation and guide for the further investigation of ancient Yahwistic poetry.

A fourth exemplar of early Israelite poetry is the Lament of David (II Samuel 1:19-27).[9] While this is a typical lamentation or Qinah, it is not composed in the elegiac rhythm of later times, but has precisely the same metrical and strophic form as the victory hymns. Its date is fixed by explicit historical references. These confirm the orthographic and linguistic indications.

In the Song of Deborah there is an enumeration of several of the tribes of Israel, with a brief characterization of each and a reference to its part in the battle with the Canaanites. These references have their origin in short "blessings", a literary genre popular in Israel especially in the period of the Judges. The blessings circulated singly or in groups, and were at some time collected and organized as a unit or set into a framework reflecting the twelve-tribe Yahwistic amphictyony. Two examples of these collections are preserved in the Old Testament, and are treated in the following studies: The Blessing of Jacob (Genesis 49), and The Blessing of Moses (Deuteronomy 33).

The analysis of the Blessings indicates that they are of approximately the same age. In each are preserved materials which antedate the eleventh century in all probability, and may be considerably older. But the Blessings as a whole reached completed form toward the end of the period of the Judges. The Blessing of Moses is of special interest, since the individual blessings have been set in a framework of high antiquity, a hymn of praise and thanksgiving. In both collections the blessings reflect the typical characteristics and representative experiences of the tribes, not particular historical events. The search for specific allusions has been largely fruitless, resulting in confusion and misunderstanding rather than in clarifying the text. General historical references without exception fit into the pre-monarchical phase of Israelite history.

Aside from the framework of the Blessing of Moses, only one other hymn of praise or thanksgiving has been included in the present series of studies: Psalm 18 = II Samuel 22. Unlike the other poems, the *terminus ad quem* for this hymn seems to be the ninth-eighth centuries B.C., as indicated by the orthographic evidence.[10] It contains much older material, however, as reflected in frequent Canaanitisms, archaic linguistic usages, and its literary and stylistic connections with the rest of the corpus of early Yahwistic poetry. The theophany in vss. 8-16 is to be grouped with those in the Song of Deborah[11], the Blessing of Moses, the Song of Miriam, and the Psalm of Habakkuk, with which it ranks in antiquity and dramatic power.[12]

The Song of Moses in Deuteronomy 32 is closely related to the compositions included in these studies. Like II Samuel 22 and several hymns in the Psalter, it is on the fringe of the corpus of ancient Israelite poetry. Despite the fact that it undeniably contains much early material, the evidence drawn from the poem itself is as yet inconclusive. For the present, therefore, the poem has been omitted. Further research seems necessary in order to determine the date and provenience of this song.

Two other groups of poetic material, not dealt with in this thesis, also properly belong to the ancient Yahwistic corpus. In the first place, there are the many poetic fragments (particularly those from the lost collections, The Book of the Wars of Yahweh, and The Book of Jashar) now embedded in the JE strata of the Tetrateuch, and in the Deuteronomic history.[13] In the second place, there is the group of so-called Canaanizing psalms. Composed at various times by Israelite poets, these hymns contain materials drawn from Canaanite sources of great antiquity. Notable examples are Psalms 29, 77, 88, 89.[14] Systematic investigation of the intricate problems connected with them must wait for another occasion.

The Metrical Structure of the Early Poems of Israel:

Since the first experimental efforts of Lowth[15], Bellermann[16], Saalshütz[17] and Ewald[18], great strides have been made in the analysis of Hebrew prosody. The intensive studies of Ley[19] and Budde[20] toward the end of the last century, and of Sievers[21] at the turn of the century, placed the subject on a solid inductive basis, which has become the departure point for all subsequent research. The investigation of comparable poetic materials from Egypt and Mesopotamia has indirectly corroborated and amplified the general findings of the German scholars; in this way basic principles applicable to the poetry of the whole ancient Near East have been established.[22] Most recently, studies in the metrical structure of early Canaanite poetry have brought to light many features of Canaanite poetic structure which are also common to early Hebrew poetry.[23] And this has brought about a new creative phase in the study of Hebrew prosody.

When due allowance is made for the differences in outlook and circumstance, in language, in literary form and content, it must nevertheless be admitted that there is a very close relationship between Ugaritic and early Hebrew poetry. The same fundamental principles governed Ugaritic and early Hebrew prosody, the reason being that the early Hebrew poets accepted the poetic canons of their more cultured neighbors. They adopted, with some modifications, the metrical patterns, characteristic imagery, and many motifs from their Canaanite models. They borrowed striking expressions, words and phrases, complete strophes and even entire poems, and adapted them, sometimes with very little change, for Israel's use.

The basic building blocks in Canaanite and early Hebrew metrical structure are the two-stress colon and the three-stress colon. The dominating principle is that of balance or symmetry: *parallelismus membrorum.* The Ugaritic texts seem mainly to be in the 3:3 pattern, as would be expected in epic poetry; but the 2:2 pattern is not uncommon, and there are numerous instances of mixed patterns of 3:3 and 2:2.[24]

In addition, a remarkable regularity obtains in the oldest Hebrew verse (as in early Canaanite poetry); this is easily recognized in spite of numerous corruptions in the preserved text.[25] This regularity lies somewhere between a simple stress meter (i.e., matching accented syllables without regard to the number of unstressed syllables), and a complex meter involving syllable count and division into metrical feet. The symmetry is exhibited chiefly in parallel cola. It rarely extends beyond this to whole strophes, nor does it apply to word or syllabic subdivisions of the colon. The strong sense of balance seems to have required the same time-length for balancing cola, i.e., approximately the same total number of syllables in each of the two cola. Since in practically all cases the number of stressed syllables would be the same, the unstressed syllables would also balance. This does not mean that there was a regular pattern of unstressed syllables in relation to stressed syllables (that is, a sequence of regular metrical feet, as suggested by Sievers), but only that there is a correspondence in the total number of unstressed syllables in parallel cola.

As already indicated the balance or equality in the number of stressed syllables has always been regarded as a fundamental principle of Hebrew metrical structure. Nevertheless, there are cases in which this balance apparently does not obtain, without however violating the canons of symmetry. It may be very difficult or impossible to assign the same number of stresses to parallel cola; at the same time they may have an equal number of syllables and balance perfectly.[26] Thus it appears that a deep sense of symmetry is the guiding principle of metrical structure, and that the stress pattern (3:3, 2:2) is only the most convenient, and generally adequate method of expressing this symmetry.

An unbalanced meter (e.g., the Qinah meter isolated by Budde, 3:2) does not appear in ancient Israelite poetry. There are examples of the 3:2 meter in Ugaritic poetry, but it does not correspond closely to the Qinah meter of later Hebrew poetry. It seems rather to be an alternate type of the "ballast variant", in which a portion of the first colon is echoed in the second, but without the customary lengthening to make up the normal syllabic balance. For the most part these "echo variants" occur singly, as interruptions in a regular 3:3 sequence: e.g.

KRT:A:12-13

'áṯṯata ṣúdqihu layapī́qu
matráḫta yúšrihu

Anat III:17-19

rī́gmu 'ī́ṯa laỵa wa-'argúmuki
háwatu wā-'aṯnīyuki

KRT:A:66-68 (cf. 160)

qâḥ(a) 'ī́mmara bayâdika
'immar(a) dâbḥi bâmā yamī́ni
lâl'a kil'atānêmi 27

Another source of imbalance in metrical structure is the extra-metrical foot, which occurs both in Ugaritic[28] and Hebrew[29] poetry. It has a special function, and stands outside the regular metrical pattern.

At the present stage of metrical studies, there still remain considerable areas of uncertainty in the analysis of early Canaanite and Hebrew poetry. The problem of vocalization is difficult, as is also that of accentuation. In the case of both languages, the general principles are well established, and a "standard" pronunciation is commonly accepted. How well this agrees with the actual vocalization of the ancient poetry, in detail, cannot be determined. In the poetry of all languages metrical considerations influence the vocalization and accentuation. How far poetic license might extend in the field of contractions, or the use of archaic, or on the other hand of colloquial forms, cannot in particular cases be decided.[30] The preservation of case endings and other archaic forms which had fallen out of popular use is well attested in Hebrew poetry, and presumably similar conditions were present in early Canaanite verse as well. Besides all this, the question of the integrity of the text is of basic importance in dealing with Hebrew poems; it is also a problem in connection with Ugaritic literature, in which a considerable period of oral (and perhaps written) transmission is involved.

There are a variety of metrical patterns in early Hebrew poetry. While the bicolon (3:3 and 2:2) is the basic unit, tricola (3:3:3 or ?2:2:2) are quite common, as in Ugaritic, and appear frequently in the corpus of ancient Hebrew verse. For the most part, tricola seem to be inserted at random in a series of bicola. Occasionally they are used in regular sequence, and even serve a structural purpose in the metrical pattern, as a climactic conclusion to the strophe.[31]

Climactic or repetitive parallelism, in a variety of forms, is a characteristic device of the oldest Israelite poetry, as also of Ugaritic.[32] It fell out of use in later Hebrew poetry, being replaced by a formal and stilted repetitiveness; thus climactic parallelism serves as an indication of the archaic nature of the poems in which it occurs. It is present in virtually all of the poetry in the corpus. It is an important feature of the Song of Miriam (Exodus 15), and reaches a peak of intricate and elaborate development in the Song of Deborah.[33]

Rhyme, which is characteristic of folk or bedouin poetry, does appear, though rarely both in Ugaritic and old Hebrew verse. Occasional examples may be found in the Canaanite epics. Thus in 68:10,

tíqqaḥu múlka ᶜālámika
dárkata dā́ta dārdā́rika [34]

and in the poetry of ancient Israel, Jud. 16:24bc[35],

nātán bᵉyadēnû šimšôn 'ôyᵉbēnû [36]
maḥrîb 'arṣēnû hirbâ ḥᵃlalênû

and others.[37]

This easily produced rhyme scheme, resulting from the repetition of the same suffix or afformative, was an inevitable feature of folk poetry, with its strongly marked beat and musical rhythm. The ready availability of the device, along with its monotonous sing-song quality, militated against its use in the sophisticated poetry of the Canaanites, or the Israelite poetry modeled upon it.[38]

Mixed metrical patterns involving bicola 3:3 and 2:2 occur both in Ugaritic and ancient Israelite poetry. Since these patterns seem to have their origin in lyric poetry, arising in connection with songs having refrains (in which the refrain will be in a different metrical arrangement than the body of the song), or antiphonal choruses, they are relatively more common in the Hebrew corpus of victory songs and hymns, than in the Ugaritic collection of epic poetry. Nevertheless, various examples may be drawn from the Ugaritic poems:

I Aqhat 44-45

šábᶜa šanāti yásruku Báᶜl(u) 3 (or 2:2)
tamānê rūkib(u) ᶜarapāti 3

bal ṭálla bal rabíba 2
bal šrᶜa tihāmtêmi 2
bal ṭbána qôl(i) Báᶜl(i) 2

68:24-26 (cf. 16-18)

yálimu kátipê zubūl(i) yám(mi) 3
bêna ᶜênê-mi ṯápiṭ(i) náhar(i) 3

yapársihu yám(mu) 2
wa-yáqil la-'árṣi 2

yinnágiṣu pinnátuhu 2
wa-yádlup tamúnuhu 2

Similar patterns occur in Accadian poetry.[39]

The mixed pattern, 3:3 and 2:2, is a characteristic feature of ancient Yahwistic poetry; and in the Victory Odes and the Lament of David it takes regular strophic form. An analysis of the strophic arrangement of these poems follows:

The Song of Deborah[40]

2

When locks were long in Israel	בפרע פרעת בישראל	3	
When volunteered the great-hearted of the people	בהתנדב <נדב>[a] עם	3	
Bless Yahweh!	ברכ יהו[b]	(2)	

3

Hear, O kings	שמע מלכמ	2	
Give ear, O princes	האזנ רזנמ	2	
I, to Yahweh	אנכ ליהו	2	AB
Even I will sing	אנכ אשר	2	AC
I will sing to Yahweh	אזמר ליהו	2	
The God of Israel	אלה ישראל	2	

---

[c] ....

17

Gilead:	גלעד[d]		
Beyond Jordan he encamps	בעבר ״ירדן שכן	3	
Dan:	דן		
Why does he take service on ships	למ יגר אנית	3	
Asher:	אשר		
He dwells at the seashore	ישב לחפ ימם	3	
And by its inlets he encamps	ועל מפרצו ישכן	3	

18

Zebulun:	זבלן		
The people scorned its life to die	עמ חרפ נפש למת	3	
Naphtali:	נפתל		
He mounted the heights of the (battle)-field	על[e] מרמ שד	3	

19

The kings came, they fought	בא מלכם נלחם	3	ABC
The kings of Canaan fought	[f]״נלחם מלכ כנען	3	CBE
At Taanach, by the waters of Megiddo	בתענך על-מ מגד	3	
Spoil of silver they did not take	בצע כסף לא לקח	3	

20

From the heavens the stars fought	מן שמם נלחם ״ככבם	3	
From their stations they fought with Sisera	ממ״לתם[g] נלחם עם ססרא	3	

21

Wadi Kishon swept them away	נחל קשן גרפם	3	ABC
Wadi Kishon overwhelmed them	[h]{נחל <קשן> קדמם[i]} / {קדמם נחל קשן}	3 / 3	ABD / DAB
His mighty chargers pounded	תדרכ״ פ<ר>ש עז[j]	3	

22

Hammered the hoofs of the horses	[]הלמ עקב ססם[k]	3	
Raced chariot-races his stallions	[l]דהר[]דהרת אברו	3	

23

Bitterly curse Meroz	אר <ארר[m]> מרז[n] [][o]	3	ABC
Bitterly curse her inhabitants	אר ארר ישבה	3	ABD
For they came not to the help of Yahweh	כ לא בא לעזרת יהו	3	ABC
To the help of Yahweh with their warriors	לעזרת יהו בגברם[p]	3	BCD

24

Blessed above women be Jael	תברך מנשם יעל [][q]	3	ABC
Above women of the tent be she blessed	מנשם באהל תברך	3	BDA

25

Water he asked	מם שאל	2	
Milk she gave	הלב נתנ	2	
In a majestic bowl	בספל אדרם	2	
She brought ghee	הקרב חמא	2	

26

Her hand to a tent-pin she put	ידה ליתד תשלחן[r]	3	
Her right hand to a workmen's wedge	˹ימנה להלמת עמלם	3	
She smote Sisera	הלמ ססרא	2	
She smashed his head	מחק ראש	2	
She struck Sisera	מחצ <ססרא>[s]	2	
She pierced his temple	חלפ רקת	2	

27

At her feet he sank, he lay flat	בן רגלה כרע[][t] שכב	3	ABC
At her feet he sank, he fell down	בן רגלה כרע נפל	3	ABD
There he sank, he fell down slain	[][u]שם ˹כרע˺ נפל שדד	3	BDE

28

Through a window peered Sisera's mother	בעד˹חלן נשקפ[v] <אם ססרא>	3	
Sisera's mother cried out through a lattice	תיבב אם ססרא בעד אשנב	3	
Wherefore tarries	מדע בשש	2	
His chariotry in coming?	רכב לבא	2	
Wherefore delay	מדע אחר	2	
The hoofs of his chariot-(horses)?	פעמ מרכבתו	2	

29

The wisest of her ladies answers her	חכמת[w] שרתה תעננ	3	
Yea, she returns words to her	אפ הא תשב אמרה לה	3	

30

Have they not found,	הלא ימצא	2
Divided the booty	יחלק שלל	2
A maid, two maids	רחם רחמתם[x]	2
For each warrior	לראש גבר[y]	2
Booty of dyed cloth for Sisera	שלל צבע-ם[z] לססרא	3 ABC
Booty of dyed cloth embroidered	שלל צבע-ם[aa] רקמ	3 ABD
Two dyed cloths embroidered, for his neck?	צבע[bb] רקמתם לצואר [][cc]	3 BDE

Notes on the Song of Deborah

a. Insert n^e*dîbî*, masculine construct plural (on the form and vocalization, see Chapter V, footnote 4), which may have dropped out by haplography. It is required by the meter, suggested by the parallel construction in the first colon. The expression occurs in Num. 21:18 and Ps. 47:10.

b. This phrase is extra-metrical, perhaps a choral response used here and at intervals throughout the song (in formal presentation).

c. Since this is a study in metrical structure, we omit verses 4-16 because of the many textual and linguistic difficulties. A number of bicola and tricola are clear, but no satisfactory continuous pattern emerges. Beginning with vs. 17, however, and continuing through vs. 23, a fairly regular series of bicola 3:3 (with one tricolon) is found.

d. A cursory examination of vs. 17-18 shows that although the meaning of MT is clear, the meter is irregular, and balance between parallel cola is lacking. If, however, the names of the tribes are set apart as extra-metrical feet, a uniform series of bicola 3:3 results. We find a similar phenomenon in the Blessings of Jacob and Moses, where the name of the tribe is not given in the Blessing itself, and therefore must have stood as an extra-metrical foot, or where the name of the tribe is given, and is plainly extra-metrical. Cf. Deut. 33:12,13; also note 46, Chapter III.

e. Read ^{c}*ālâ*; in early orthography the final vowel would not have been indicated. A verb is required both for reasons of meter and sense. For the idiom cf. II Kings 19:23 = Isa. 37:24. עָל <ל>מרם is also possible, cp. Ps. 68:19.

f. Omit for metrical reasons. Its presence impairs the symmetry of the bicolon, abc:cbd.

g. Read *mimmazz*^{e}*lôtām*, "from their stations", following Winckler and other commentators. The change *z* > *s* may be due to an error in oral transmission. Cp. now KRT A:99,188, *mzl*.

h. The text is a conflate of two early variants. One apparently read נחל <קשן> קדמם, *qîšôn* having fallen out as a result of homoioarkton. The other variant read קדמם נחל קשן.

i. Read here probably, *qidd*^{e}*mām*, "confronted them", following the commentators. Note a similar usage of this root in II Sam.22:6,19 = Ps. 18:6,19. The order of the cola may have been reversed, but it is not necessary to impose a strictly logical pattern in poetry of this kind.

j. As it stands, this passage does not fit into the context at all; cf. Burney, *ad loc*. However, by connecting it with the two cola which follow, reading the consonantal text in accordance with the principles of early orthography, and making a single insertion in the preserved text, an eminently satisfactory colon results: תדרכנפ<ר>שעז, *tidr*^{e}*kan(na) paršê* ^{c}*uzzô*, "his mighty chargers pounded (the ground)". The first word, *tidr*^{e}*kan(na)*, is the third feminine singular used with a plural or collective subject. On the occurrence of this form in biblical passages, cf. Albright, "The Old Testament and the Canaanite Language and Literature", *CBQ* 7 (1945), 22-23; Chapter III, note 84; Chapter IV, note 55. The reading *paršê* is suggested by the parallels in vs. 22a and b. It is to be noted that in early Hebrew epigraphy, *resh* and *pe* are very much alike; the *resh* may have fallen out through a haplographic confusion of the letters. With respect to ^{c}*uzzô*, the final *ô* of the suffix would not have been indicated in the orthography of the tenth century. Its presence is indicated by the parallel אביריו.

k. Read *sûsîm*; the *mem* has been displaced; so LXX (A). This is adopted by most commentators.

l. On the reconstruction of this colon, cf. Albright, "The Song of Deborah in the Light of Archaeology", *BASOR* #62 (1936), p. 30.

m. Read *'ôrû 'ārôr* as in the third colon; on the structure of the verse, cf. vs. 12a. *'ārôr* has dropped out by haplography; in the early orthography the *matres lectionis* would not have appeared. Burney arrives at a similar reconstruction in a somewhat different fashion; cf. also Sievers, *Metrische Studien I, Studien zur hebräischen Metrik*, Leipzig, 1901, *ad loc.*, and Slotki, "The Song of Deborah", *JTS* 33 (1932), pp. 345-46.

n. The reading of MT is problematical. Cf. Albright, "The Earliest Forms of Hebrew Verse", *JPOS* II (1922), p. 79, n. 5, and "Some Additional Notes on the Song of Deborah", *JPOS* II (1922), pp. 284-85; also Alt, "Meros (Jud. 5:23)", *ZAW* 57 (1940-41), pp. 244-47.

o. The second colon is an interpolation. The poetic structure of vs. 23a is abc:abd, for 23b, abc:bcd.

p. Read probably *b^{e}-gibbōremô*, "with their warriors". The final *ô* would not have been indicated in early orthography.

q. As commonly recognized, this passage is also an interpolation, cf. Jud. 4:17. The poetic pattern is abc:bda.

r. Read *tišlaḥan(na)*, second feminine singular with the energic *nun* but without the pronominal suffix; cf. Burney, *ad loc.* This form of the imperfect is not uncommon in early Hebrew poetry. Cf. Albright, "The Oracles of Balaam", p. 212, n. 23; Chapter III, n. 67; Chapter IV, note 25; "Song of Deborah", n. j.

s. The metrical pattern requires a measure here; the simplest emendation is to insert סטרא, in parallel with the first colon of the section.

t. The text of the first colon is conflate, *šākab* and *nāpal* being the variant readings. Since the second colon is also preserved separately, with *nāpal*, it is clear that *šākab* stood originally in the first colon. Logically, perhaps, they ought to be reversed; but the third colon indicates that the order adopted here is correct.

u. Omit *ba'^{a}šer*, as prosaic and extra-metrical. This insertion has resulted in the displacement of *šām*, which belongs at the head of the colon.

v. The reconstruction of vs. 28a is based upon the evidence of the different Greek mss. The structure of MT shows that the verbal forms are to be separated and assigned to each of the two cola. This leaves the first colon too short, and in any case a reference to the mother of Sisera is needed. Since LXX (A) actually reads ἡ μήτηρ Σισαρα in the first colon (though the second colon is corrupt), that becomes the likeliest emendation.

w. Read the singular, following the versions, and as indicated in the context.

x. The enumerative device is typical of old Canaanite poetry. Note the parallel in vs. 30, cf. footnote z. The use of the dual in both instances is archaic, and finds a parallel in the extensive use of the dual in Ugaritic. In later Hebrew the dual was restricted to parts of the body occurring in pairs, and other natural pairs.

y. Read *gibbôr*, following LXX (A); this is indicated by the context, and also improves the meter.

z. The enumerative device is again in operation. The use of the dual in the third colon indicates that the singular is required here. Read *ṣêba*^{c}*-m* absolute singular with enclitic *mem*.

aa. Read here *ṣêba*^{c}*-m riqmâ*, "a piece of embroidered dye-stuff". This is a construct chain, in which enclitic *mem* is attached to the construct. On this form, cf. Albright, "The Oracles of Balaam", p. 219, n. 83; "The Old Testament and Canaanite Language", pp. 22-23.

bb. Read the dual construct, **ṣab*^{c}*ê riqmātêm*, "two pieces of embroidered dye-stuff". The final vowel would not be indicated in early Hebrew orthography.

cc. Read *ṣawwā'ro*, "his neck", following the LXX. Omit the final *šālāl*, which is hypermetrical. It has come in through the influence of the same word in each of the two preceding cola. Needless to say, the extensive use of repetition in the original poem presented considerable difficulties to the scribes in the course of transmission. Both the omission of elements meant to be repeated, and the repetition of materials not so intended would result. It is surprising that in considerable sections, the text has been preserved in excellent order.

The metrical structure of the Song of Deborah may be described as follows. The introductory section consists of strophes with the pattern:

3:3
2:2
2:2
2:2

There is a possible variation in the number of bicola 2:2. The main body of the poem is narrative in style, and seems to follow the standard 3:3 pattern. The strophes seem to be irregular in length, and are not sharply distinguished from each other.[41] The latter part of the surviving portion of the poem consists of two well-defined strophes, with an elaborate structure (vs. 24-30). The pattern is:

vs. 24-27	vs. 28-30
3:3	3:3
2:2 2:2	2:2 2:2
3:3	3:3
2:2 2:2	2:2 2:2
3:3:3	3:3:3

The same mixed meter, 3:3 and 2:2, occurs in the Song of Miriam[42], but the strophic arrangement is somewhat different.[43] Easily discernible in this poem are three distinct structural ele-elements: a) a bicolon 3:3;[44] b) a couplet of bicola 2:2.2:2;[45] c) a trio of bicola 2:2.2:2.2:2.[46] Each strophe apparently consists of a grouping of three units: the thread of the story is carried by the trio, while the couplet and bicolon serve generally as either introduction or conclusion, and consist of a refrain or summary of the action described in the trio.[47] There are five complete strophes in the poem, along with introductory sentence and conclusion.

The Lament of David

With respect to metrical structure, the Lament of David belongs to the same group of poems.[48] Its strophic pattern is somewhat simpler, however, consisting of a series of stanzas in 2:2 meter, interspersed with bicola 3:3. The chief source of difficulty is the refrain, which originally occurred in a number of different forms. Different versions of it are embedded in the corrupt passages, vss. 19,25; only a single example has been preserved intact, the 3:3 bicolon in vs. 27:

'êkâ nāp^e lû gibbôrîm
yôb^e dû k^e lê milḥāmâ

How have the warriors fallen
Perished the weapons of war!

It seems probable that the refrain in every case began with the same colon: *'êkâ nāp^e lû gibbôrîm*, but was joined to one of several alternate second cola, depending upon its place in the poem. Some of these second cola are now preserved in vss. 19 and 25. It is possible that a tricolon was used in some cases. Since the lament in Hebrew poetry normally begins with the word *'êk(â)*, it is a plausible suggestion that the poem was introduced by the refrain. Whether some form of it was used with every strophe, or only after certain strophes or how many varieties of the refrain there were, or whether the same one was used more than once, are all matters of speculation.

Six strophes make up the body of the Lament. The first two consist of four bicola 2:2, the remaining four strophes of three bicola 2:2. In a number of cases the normal parallelism between cola is to be observed (so vs. 22a, 23c, etc.); in a larger number of instances parallelism obtains between bicola, rather than cola (so vs. 20, 22bc, 24bc). This development can be described as a variation on the basic 2:2 pattern, in which the cola are lumped together to form the equivalent of a 4:4:4(:4) strophic arrangement. The net effect is a subtle slowing up of the staccato speed of the 2:2 pattern of the war songs; a dignified and solemn movement, suitable to the mood of the Qinah, results.

The Lament of David

I

Tell it not   20   אל תגד
In the squares of Gath,   ב<רחבת>[a] גת

Proclaim it not   אל תבשר
In the streets of Ashkelon,   בחצת אשקלן

Lest they rejoice,   פן תשלחנ
The Philistine maidens,   בנת פלשתם

Lest they exult,   פן תעלזנ
The daughters of the heathen.   בנת [b]⸢י⸣ערלם

II

O mountain of Gilboa   21   הר[c] בגלבע
Nor dew, nor rain   אל טל [d]⸢י⸣אל מטר

....
[e] ....

For there was defiled   כ שם נגעל
The warriors' shield,   מגן גברם

The shield of Saul   מגן שאל
Not anointed with oil.   בל משח בשמן[f]

III

From the blood of the slain,   22   מדם חללם
From the bowels of warriors,   מחלב גברם

The bow of Jonathan   קשת [g]ינתן
Turned not back,   לנשג אחר

And the sword of Saul   וחרב שאל
Returned not empty.   לא תשב רקם

	IV	
Saul and Jonathan	23	שאל ו ינתן
Beloved, gracious,		[h]˹י˺נאהבם ˹י˺נעמם
In life and in death		בחיהם ובמתם
They were not parted		לא נפרד[i]
They were swifter than eagles,		מנשרם קל
They were stronger than lions.		מארית גבר
	V	
O daughters of Israel	24	בנת ישראל
For Saul weep ye		אל שאל בכנ
....		
....		
....		
[j].........		
	VI	
I grieve over thee	26	צר ל עלך
My brother Jonathan;		אח ינתן
Thou wast my great delight,		נעמת לי מאד
Wonderful wast thou;		נפלא [k]<א>ת
To love thee was for me		אהבתך לי
Better than the love of women.		מאהבת נשם

Notes on the Lament of David

a. The two bicola of vs. 20a clearly do not balance, cf. Albright, "The Earliest Forms of Hebrew Verse", p. 84. Comparison with the bicola of vs. 20b shows that the first bicolon of 20a is defective, and not that the second is hypermetrical. The missing word in 20a is in all probability רחבת; note the very striking parallel in Amos 5:16b, *b^e kol r^e ḥōbôt mispēd ūb^e kol ḥûṣôt yôm^e rû hô hô.*

b. Omit the article in accordance with the canons of early Hebrew poetic style.

c. Read here the singular *hari*, with the genitive case ending; in every other occurrence of this expression the singular is used. The preservation of the case ending in the *nomen regens* of a construct chain is not uncommon in early Hebrew poetry. On the appearance of the preposition in the construct chain, cf. GK §130a. The origin of the peculiar construction here may be found in the two different expressions occurring in I and II Samuel: *har haggilbō̄ac* (= *har gilbō̄ac* of I Chronicles), and simply *baggilbō̄ac*.

d. Omit the conjunction, *metri causa*. Note that in a closely parallel passage in Ugaritic the conjunction does not appear, I Aqhat 44: bl . ṭl . bl . rbb . Cf. Ginsberg, "A Ugaritic Parallel to II Sam 1:21", *JBL* LVII (1938), pp. 209-213.

e. This bicolon is corrupt, as recognized by all scholars. The only metrical point to be noted is that as the line stands it is probably defective. For a valuable but not completely convincing suggestion, cf. Ginsberg, "A Ugaritic Parallel to II Sam 1:21", p. 213.

f. Read *bal mušaḥ bešamn*; *mušaḥ* is the qal passive perfect, with the adverb *bal*. The longer form *b^e lî* is normally used only with nominal forms, while *bal* is restricted to verbal forms. In early orthography, both forms would have been written בל. On the idiom, cf. Isa. 21:5.

g. The name was undoubtedly pronounced *yônātān* in the Northern dialect, at this time.

h. Omit the article here, and before the next word; cf. footnote b.

i. There is a serious metrical difficulty in this bicolon; it cannot be divided satisfactorily into two balancing cola. Nevertheless, the bicolon as a unit balances perfectly with the preceding and following bicola. This suggests that we have here a real variant of the bicolon 2:2, namely an equivalent four-accent colon.

j. The general meaning of the passage is clear, but there are difficulties connected with the detailed interpretation of the various elements. The metrical pattern, presumably a couplet of bicola 2:2, is somewhat irregular as well, and points to a certain disarrangement of the text.

k. This anomalous formation is probably the result of the loss of an *aleph* by haplography. Read נפלא <א>ת, "surpassing wast thou". This supplies a parallel to the previous colon, and clears up the metrical problem.

Archaic Characteristics of the Grammar, Vocabulary and Style:

The body of poetry which comes from early Israelite times is distinguished by characteristic archaisms. In the morphology of the verb a number of archaic forms have been isolated. One of the more important is the so-called *t*-form imperfect used with duals or collectives. It was first identified in the Ugaritic literature, and subsequently in the Amarna correspondence and Israelite poetry.[49] Examples occur in Deut. 33:16[50] and Gen. 49:26.[51] Note other occurrences in Hab. 3:3,9,16.[52] The energic *nun* was a living form in ancient Yahwistic poetry. It occurs in all imperfect forms, and not only, as in later Hebrew, in plural forms in -*û*, or before pronominal suffixes. Examples appear in the Oracles of Balaam[53], the Blessing of Jacob[54], the Song of Deborah[55], and the Blessing of Moses.[56] In addition there are a number of isolated archaic forms such as *ša-qamtî* (Jud. 5:7), a second person feminine singular[57]; or a possible infixed-*t* form in Deut. 33:3.[58]

The most striking feature of the morphology of the noun is the frequent preservation of old case endings.[59] The survival of the case endings is due in almost every case to clear-cut metrical requirements. It is to be presumed that many more case endings were present in the original form of these poems, especially in those instances in which metrical considerations enter, but that these were lost in the process of textual transmission and revision.

The persistence of archaic forms of the pronominal suffixes is another feature of the old poetry. The regular use of -*mô* <(-*mû* < -*himmŭ̄*) in Ex. 15 is a parade example.[60] There is also some evidence for the occasional occurrence of other old formations such as **liyă̄* and **lahû*.[61] The survival of the longer forms of the pronominal suffixes (e.g., -*kă̄* // -*k*; -*kĭ̄* // -*k*; *hēmma* // *hēm*) was due in part at least to metrical considerations.[62]

In a similar way, longer and shorter forms of many particles existed side by side, the choice in particular cases being dictated by the metrical requirements of the colon. Thus, for example: *'êk* // *'êkâ*; *hēn* // *hinnê*[63]; etc., prepositions, *ᶜal* // *ᶜălê*; *ᶜad* // *ᶜădê*; and so on.

The old poems preserve a number of particles which exhibit archaic features. Thus there is the use of the preposition *b* in the sense, "from" (= *min*) as in Ugaritic.[64] Examples occur in the hymn, II Sam. 22 = Ps. 18, vss. 9,14,16.[65] The particle *l*, "O!", seems to appear in Ps. 68:34, and may occur elsewhere in the corpus.[66] The particle (ה)הם = Ugar. *hm*, "Behold!", appears in Deut. 33:17.[67] Quite common in these studies is the use of the enclitic *-m* (= *mi* of the Amarna letters and Ugaritic texts).[68] The enclitic *-m* may appear with prepositions (e.g., *'ittô-m*, Dt. 33:2), with a noun in the absolute state (e.g., *'ēl-m*, Num. 23:22), with a noun in the construct state[69] (e.g., *motnê-m qamiw*, Deut. 33:11, and *'apîqî-m yām*, II Sam. 22:16 = Ps. 18:16), and with verbs (e.g., תמלא-ם and תרש-ם in Ex. 15:9).[70]

The syntax of the poems exhibits certain peculiarities. The article is not used as a rule, and when it is, it retains its older demonstrative force. The sign of the definite direct object, את, and the relative pronoun, אשר, also do not appear in authentic old Hebrew poetry. The relative clause is introduced, occasionally by *zû* (Ex. 15:13,16), or ש (Jud. 5:7, Num. 24:3)[71] or, without the use of the relative particle, by simply placing the two clauses in juxtaposition (Num. 23:8 bis, Ex. 15:2 bis, Gen. 49:27). The participle may also serve as a surrogate for a relative construction as in later Hebrew.

The syntax of the verb in ancient Yahwistic poetry (especially the use of *qtl* and *yqtl* forms) corresponds much more closely to that of Ugaritic poetry, than to Hebrew prose or late poetry. The *yqtl* form is vari-temporal[72] in usage, expressing past time as well as future time; it often appears (without the conjunction) in consecutive sequence with *qtl* forms, with a past meaning. There is abundant evidence in our studies to show that old Yahwistic poetry was governed by the same syntactic pattern. Examples of the use of the *yqtl* form without the *waw*-conversive in parallel with *qtl* forms are found throughout the corpus. Note especially instances in Jud. 5:17 bis, 25-26,28; Ex. 15:5, 12,14,15; and II Sam. 22 = Ps. 18:7,12,14,16,39 bis,44.[73] There can be no doubt that in this corpus of poetry the time-aspect of the *yqtl* form was determined by the context, and not the presence or absence of the so-called *waw*-conversive. In other words, old Hebrew poetry reflects a stage of the language which preceded the final development of the standard *waw*-conversive sequence. This observation has been obscured by the fact that in the course of the transmission of the text of these poems, the conjunction has been introduced at the beginning of cola in many places where it did not originally belong.[74] In some of these cases the conjunction was attached to a *yqtl* verb form, thus producing, in effect, a *waw*-conversive form. That this superficial conformity to the standard prose practice of the Bible is without real significance is made clear by a careful comparison of parallel passages, especially in II Sam. 22 and Ps. 18.[75] The conjunction has been introduced haphazardly, and the alternation of *qtl* and *yqtl* forms is an independent phenomenon.[76]

The early Israelite poems have close lexicographic affinities with each other and with the Ugaritic literature. This interlocking vocabulary includes a number of words which recur regularly in our poems, but which tend to die out of use (except as conscious archaisms) in later Hebrew literature. The following examples are common in ancient Israelite poetry, and also occur in Ugaritic: רבץ, קדקד, ראם, אדר, בני אלים, נער, שכן ("encamp"), דאה, קנה ("create"), אבר, במה ("back"). Other terms, used frequently in early Hebrew poetry, but not appearing in the Ugaritic literature are: צעד, מחקק, and כחש.

There are a number of words in old Hebrew poetry, also occurring in Ugaritic, the meaning of which has been elucidated by their usage in Ugaritic. Examples are: בשן, "serpent" = *baṯnu*; דבא, "strength" (cf. *db'at*); ערפת, "clouds" (cf. *rākib ᶜarapāti*); חשרת, "strainer" = *ḫṯr*; עלי, "the Exalted One" (cf. *ᶜly*); כשרת, "female singers" (cf. *kôṯar*); גפן, "harness = *gapnu*; מן, "whoever" = *man*.

Certain parallel expressions are used repeatedly throughout the old Hebrew poetic corpus, e.g., מים רבים; שור // ראם; אהל // משכן; ראש // קדקד; הררי קדם // גבעת עולם; אויב // קם.

This sampling of the archaic features of the grammar, vocabulary and style of the ancient Israelite poetry will suffice to demonstrate the intimate relationships which the poems have among themselves and to the earlier body of Ugaritic literature.

Archaic Orthography in Early Hebrew Poetry:[77]

The present Massoretic text of the early Yahwistic poems is the final stage in a history of scribal transmission that covers 2000 years. During this period many changes occurred in the spelling practices of Israel. At regular intervals the biblical texts were revised in accordance with the then-current orthographic principles. In spite of the most persistent efforts of scribes and grammarians, the orthography of the Old Testament was never completely standardized; and clear evidence of each of the earlier stages in the development of Hebrew spelling has been preserved in the received text.[78] Thus the Hebrew Bible which tradition has delivered to us is in reality a palimpsest: underlying the visible text, the various spelling customs of older ages have been recorded.

The need for an adequate treatment of the evolution of Hebrew orthography has long been recognized, as well as its important value in textual analysis and reconstruction, and the dating of biblical materials. Sufficient inscriptional materials, properly dated and interpreted, to permit such an inductive analysis of Northwest Semitic orthography, have only recently been made available to the scholarly world. The broad outlines of Hebrew orthographic development are now quite clear. A brief sketch follows.

The evidence for an original principle of phonetic consonantism in Northwest Semitic orthographic practice seems to be conclusive. The principle was inherent in the Proto-Canaanite alphabet; and the South Semitic and Ugaritic systems of writing developed under the influence of the same principle. A system of purely consonantal writing persisted in Phoenician until very late times, with a minimum of historical spelling. In Hebrew the principle of phonetic consonantism was followed down to the tenth century B.C., first through the use of the Proto-Canaanite alphabet, then under the direct influence of Phoenician spelling. This circumstance, a logical inference from the history of the Israelites and their cultural and commercial relations in the tenth century, is confirmed by the orthography of the Gezer Calendar.[79]

The epigraphic evidence for Hebrew orthography indicates that before the ninth century, Hebrew was written in a purely consonantal script. In agreement with Phoenician principles of spelling, final vowels were not indicated in the orthography. Inscriptional data from the early period is limited, but examples of this defective writing are to be found in the Gezer Calendar.[80]

The phonemic character of the old script had both advantages and disadvantages. It was a very simple method of writing, easily learned, and readily adapted to the needs of almost any language. It lent itself to phonetic writing and reflected with great sensitivity dialectal variations and phonological changes. Regular revisions in the orthography eliminated the confusion created by historical spellings. On the other hand, as Northwest Semitic continued to break down, purely consonantal writing became a more and more ambiguous form of shorthand, and in the long run had to be abandoned.

The first important modification in the Phoenician orthographic system was made, apparently by the Aramaeans, shortly after they borrowed the alphabet (ca. 11th century B.C.). Besides adapting the alphabet to the representation of non-Phoenician phonemes (by their closest equivalent in the Phoenician alphabet), they radically altered the basic principles of spelling. A system was developed for the indication of final vowels by the signs for consonants, which were homogeneous with the vowel sounds: thus *yodh* for final *i*, *waw* for final *u*, and *he* for the remaining sounds in the language. The precise manner in which the system of *matres lectionis* originated is still uncertain. It is clear, however, that there was not sufficient time between the borrowing of the Phoenician alphabet and the development of the system for it to have grown spontaneously out of historical spellings. Moreover, the tendency in Phoenician writing (as also in Aramaic) was to eliminate historical spellings, not preserve them. Rather, we must suppose conscious invention, and elaboration in the use of vowel letters. Isolated examples of historical spelling may have suggested the use of vowel letters (e.g., **-iya* > **-iy* > *î*, with the *yodh* preserved). The consistent representation of all final vowels is the result of standardization. The same system which had been introduced by the Aramaeans was also used by the Moabites and Israelites from the ninth century on. It is probable that the center of radiation was Aram.

Some time after the end of the tenth century (probably by the middle of the ninth century, to judge from the Mesha Inscription), a system of final *matres lectionis* was introduced into Hebrew; and from that time on, all final vowels were indicated in the orthography (in both Northern and Southern dialects).

The scheme adopted was the same as that used in Aramaic and Moabite:

The final vowel *i* was represented by *yodh*.

The final vowel *u* was represented by *waw*.

The final vowels *a*, *e*, *o*, were all represented by *he*.

Final vowels are uniformly indicated in the orthography of the ninth century and following, medial vowels uniformly not. The few exceptions, where medial *matres lectionis* seem to appear, all date from the sixth century. Since internal vowel letters had already appeared sporadically in Aramaic inscriptions more than 100 years earlier, the possibility of their use in Hebrew must be recognized. None of the examples, however, is absolutely certain.

While there is relatively little epigraphic evidence from the northern part of Palestine, dialectal differences are discernible. The most important of these for orthographic analysis is the contraction of diphthongs in all positions: *ay* > *ê*, *aw* > *ô*. In the Southern dialect, however, diphthongs remained uncontracted in all positions (down to the exile). The diphthong *ay* was represented by its consonantal element *yodh*; the diphthong *aw* was represented by *waw*.

Since the system of *matres lectionis* was apparently not used in Hebrew before the ninth century, and since that system was identical with the system used in Aramaic from the beginning of that century, if not earlier, and in Moabite from the middle of the ninth century at the latest, it can hardly be doubted that this system was borrowed by the Israelites from the Aramaeans during the course of the ninth century. The common explanation that the Hebrew system of vowel letters was an indigenous development, arising gradually out of an accumulation of historical spellings, does not square with the epigraphic evidence. Rather, the divergence in Hebrew orthography from the traditional phonetic consonantism of Old Canaanite and Phoenician (as illustrated in the tenth century inscriptions from Byblos)[81], came about through the adoption of a system of *matres lectionis* already in existence.

The later phases in the evolution of Hebrew orthography are more complex than the earlier ones. From the exile to the Herodian period there was a general increase in the use of internal *matres lectionis*. With the contraction of unaccented medial diphthongs, *yodh* and *waw* (preserved by historical spelling) received the new values *ê* and *ô* respectively; the use of *waw* with this value was extended to the final position, where it gradually replaced *he* as the sign for *ô*. During the same period, *aleph* quiesced generally, and was pressed into service as a *mater lectionis*.[82] The fullest development of *plene* writing was reached apparently during the Maccabaean Era.[83] This is clearly reflected in the orthography of the first of the newly discovered Isaiah mss., and other documents from the same find.[84]

Alongside this development, a more conservative orthographic tradition was maintained. The moderately *plene* spelling of the early post-exilic period is reflected in the second of the Isaiah mss.[85] During the succeeding Rabbinic period, strenuous efforts were made to fix the orthography of the biblical text. This was done on the basis of the mss. preserving the more conservative orthography. The result was, by and large, a biblical text in the spelling of the Persian period, still containing some traces of both earlier and later practices.

In the following period of scribal activity, this became the standard text, and a uniform orthography was thus imposed upon all the books of the canon. Evidence for this is to be found in the transliterations of the Hebrew text in the work of Origen and Jerome, and also in the Palestinian fragments from the period of earliest Massoretic activity. This process of standardization not only eliminated the real orthographic peculiarities of the divergent Maccabaean tradition, but also many of the valid longer forms of the suffixes, afformatives, adverbs, and other particles. This is clear from the first Isaiah ms. which preserves a number of archaic poetical forms which no longer appear in the Massoretic text. It is interesting to observe that the Massoretes restored a few of the longer forms in vocalizing the consonantal text (e.g., ךָ-, ןָ-, מָ-, etc.), apparently on the basis of old mss. in the Maccabaean tradition in their possession.[86]

A knowledge of the evolution of Hebrew orthography is important for the accurate analysis of biblical texts. Many obscure, corrupt, and difficult passages have been clarified when it was recognized that archaic spelling features were preserved in them, having in some way escaped revision. It is also possible to identify traces of ancient orthographic strata in a composition, and thus, in principle, to fix a *terminus ad quem* (i.e., the end of the period during which those orthographic principles were actually used) for the writing down of the material in question. In practice, however, orthographic analysis is beset by a multitude of complicating factors, a situation which might have been expected in dealing with a text which has passed through centuries of scribal transmission.

In the first place, orthographic analysis is of practically no value in determining the date of clear, easily understood passages, especially in the prose of the Bible. In such cases orthographic revision has been so thorough as to eliminate almost all traces of older spelling practices. The few "archaisms" which may survive, are generally to be explained as resulting from scribal error, or artificial intrusion.[87] In the second place, the results of orthographic analysis, even in those areas where it may be applied successfully, are generally hedged with subjective considerations and therefore have an element of uncertainty. This derives from the fact that archaic spelling is, as a rule, still preserved in the Hebrew text only in difficult or corrupt passages.[88] Hence reinterpretation, reconstruction and emendation are frequently necessary in order to produce an intelligible text. Since the reconstruction is generally made on the assumption of an archaic orthography (based upon a presumed date for the poem), the case for archaic orthography in particular instances will depend upon the validity of the reconstruction.

These factors dictate a policy of caution in using orthographic analysis in connection with old Hebrew poetry. Instances of archaic spelling must be sufficiently concentrated in a given piece to outweigh the possibility of error, coincidence, and artificial reintroduction as an explanation of the present text; there is also the subjective element in reconstructing the text to contend with. In the studies which follow, orthographic analysis has served to corroborate the date assigned to a poem, rather than fix it. In the case of II Sam. 22 = Psalm 18, for example, analysis provided only scattered instances of spellings characteristic of pre-ninth century Israel. On the other hand, the hymn preserves a considerable number of spellings typical of the ninth-eighth century (in the Northern dialect), indicating rather clearly that the poem was in written form during this period. The poem is therefore reconstructed in the orthography of the later period; though this does not rule out the possibility of earlier written or oral composition. The other poems in the corpus are reconstructed in the orthography of the tenth century because there is more impressive orthographic evidence, and other strong indications of early date.

In sum, the use of orthographic analysis has proved extraordinarily valuable in the clarification and emendation of difficult passages in old Hebrew poetry; only in an auxiliary capacity has it proved useful in determining the date of the written text of early Israelite poems.

Footnotes

1. W. F. Albright, "The Oracles of Balaam", *JBL* LXIII (1944), pp. 207-233.

2. Cf. W. F. Albright, "The Old Testament and the Canaanite Language and Literature", *CBQ* 7 (1945), pp. 5-31.

3. C. F. Burney, *The Book of Judges*, London, 1918.

4. Albright, "The Earliest Forms of Hebrew Verse", *JPOS* II (1922), pp. 69-86.

5. For bibliography, see note 40.

6. For the details of reconstruction and interpretation, see the treatment of this poem in Chapter II.

7. See the discussion in S. R. Driver, *The Book of Exodus* (*The Cambridge Bible for Schools and Colleges*), Cambridge, 1911, pp. 129ff. The antiquity, even Mosaic date, of the refrain, vs. 21, is recognized by all. The older scholars defended an early date for part of the poem, perhaps as far as vs. 10; in recent times, it is being increasingly recognized that the poem is a unit, however. Cf. R. H. Pfeiffer, *Introduction to the Old Testament*, New York, 1941 (2nd ed. 1948), p. 281; also A. H. McNeile, *The Book of Exodus* (*Westminster Commentaries*), 2nd ed., London, 1917, pp. 88ff. Note also the comments of P. Haupt in "Moses' Song of Triumph", *AJSL* XX (1903-04), pp. 150-154.

8. This is based partly upon a new analysis of the route of the Exodus by Albright, "Exploring in Sinai with the University of California African Expedition", *BASOR* #109 (1948), pp. 13-16. The bearing of the song on the problem of the crossing of the Reed Sea will be discussed in a forthcoming study by Prof. Albright.

9. See below for a brief treatment of this poem.

10. See the detailed treatment of this psalm in Chapter V.

11. The same theophany, with minor variations, is also recorded in Ps. 68:8-9 (on this poem see footnote 12).

12. Prof. Albright's forthcoming studies of Hab. 3 and Ps. 68 show that these pieces contain a high proportion of early materials which belong to the corpus of ancient Yahwistic poetry. We are indebted to Prof. Albright for making available to us the results of these studies. In addition much material for this dissertation has been gathered in seminars conducted by Prof. Albright dealing with II Sam. 22 = Ps. 18, and Ps. 68.

13. Because of their fragmentary nature these pieces are not susceptible to the kind of analysis undertaken in these studies. Occasional striking bits of evidence are to be found, and references to these will be found in the body of the dissertation.

14. Studies by Ginsberg, Gaster, Patton and others (see the bibliography for references) have greatly increased our

understanding of these psalms. Canaanite materials are to be found in other psalms as well, and occasional reminiscences and allusions throughout the Psalter.

15. R. Lowth, *Lectures on the Sacred Poetry of the Hebrews*, (trans. by G. Gregory), Andover, 1829.

16. J. J. Bellermann, *Versuch über die Metrik der Hebräer*, Berlin, 1813.

17. J. L. Saalshütz, *Form und Geist der biblisch-hebräischen Poesie*, Königsberg, 1853.

18. H. Ewald, *Die Dichter des Alten Bundes*, 2nd ed., Göttingen, Vol. I, 1866; Vol. II, 1867; Vol. III, 1854 (bound with Vol. II).

19. J. Ley, *Die metrischen Formen der hebräischen Poesie*, Leipzig, 1866; *Gründzüge des Rhythmus, des Vers- und Strophenbaues in der hebräischen Poesie*, Halle, 1875; *Leitfaden der Metrik der hebräischen Poesie*, Halle, 1887.

20. K. Budde, "Das hebräische Klagelied", *ZAW* 2 (1882), pp. 1-52.

21. E. Sievers, *Metrische Studien. I: Studien zur hebräischen Metrik*, Leipzig, 1901; II: *Die hebräischen Genesis*, Leipzig, 1904.

22. Cf. Albright, "The Earliest Forms of Hebrew Verse", pp. 69-73.

23. For a brief review of the recent literature, see J. H. Patton, *Canaanite Parallels in the Book of Psalms*, Baltimore, 1944, pp. 1-12.

24. See below the analysis of the Song of Deborah and the Lament of David.

25. This regularity is common to ancient Israelite and Canaanite poetry, but tends to disappear in later prophetic oracles and psalms.

26. Certain instances of Gordon's "ballast variant" (cf. *Ugaritic Handbook*, Rome, 1947, I, 13:107) fall into this category. Occasionally, it is exceedingly difficult to determine whether a particular metrical pattern is 3:3 or 2:2, as for example in Gen. 49:7, 17; the symmetry is nevertheless apparent.

27. As the text stands, the third colon is considerably shorter. However, it may be defective, since a preposition *b* or *bm* is needed.

28. Cf. H. L. Ginsberg, "The Rebellion and Death of Ba^{c}lu", *Orientalia* V (1936), pp. 171ff.

29. Cf. Chapter III, footnote 46; also "The Song of Deborah", footnote d.

30. Cases of poetic contractions in Accadian verse have been isolated by Prof. Albright (private communication); a number of probable instances occur in early Israelite poetry; cf. Chapter IV, notes 71, 82.

31. Note the structure of Deut. 33:2-3, three tricola 3:3:3; cf. Chapter IV, note 1. On the structure of the Song of Deborah, see the treatment included in this chapter.

32. Burney identified the characteristic features of climactic parallelism in the Song of Deborah, cf. *The Book of Judges, ad loc.* Ginsberg, "The Rebellion and Death of Ba^c^lu", p. 180, described the particular forms of this device in Ugaritic poetry, and then discovered the same forms in biblical verse. Working from this basis, Albright has thoroughly investigated this structural type in his treatment of the "Psalm of Habakkuk".

33. For details see the treatment of the Song of Deborah in this chapter, and the study of the Song of Miriam in Chapter II.

34. Cf. Albright, *JBL* LXII (1942), p. 117.

35. The text has been restored on the basis of the variants in vs. 23 and 24. Features of prose writing, like the sign of the accusative and the relative pronoun have been eliminated. In addition, the word *'^e^lôhênû* in the first colon has been dropped for metrical reasons. Apparently the text is a conflate, on which see footnote 36.

36. As it stands the bicolon is of the form 3:2, in disagreement with the second bicolon which is 2:2. The *-ênû* ending of *'^e^lôhênû* shows that it stood as the second and last element in a colon; working from this, we may reconstruct a variant reading of the first bicolon:

nātan '^e^lôhênû šimšôn b^e^yadēnû

37. Other examples of rhyme are to be found in the Song of Lamech (Gen. 4:23-24), and Genesis 49:3, cf. Chapter III, note 6. See also Albright, "The Earliest Forms of Hebrew Verse", p. 86 in connection with Num. 21:27ff.

38. Milton's strong comments on rhyme in English poetry would have met with the approval of the Israelite bard.

39. Cf. Albright, "The Earliest Forms of Hebrew Verse", pp. 69-73; also "The Psalm of Habakkuk", *passim*.

40. For recent bibliography on the Song of Deborah, see T. Piatti, "Una nuova interpretazione metrica, testuale, esegetica, del Cantico di Debora (Giudici 5:2-31)", *Biblica* 27 (1946), pp. 207-209. In addition to the works cited in footnotes 3 and 4, there are a number of other studies of varying value and significance, among them Haupt's "Die Schlacht von Taanach", *Studien zur semitischen Philologie und Religionsgeschichte* (*Julius Wellhausen Festschrift*) ed. by K. Marti, *Beihefte z. ZAW* 27 (1914), pp. 191-225; G. F. Moore, *A Critical and Exegetical Commentary on on Judges* (*ICC*), New York, 1895, pp. 127-173; J. Pedersen, *Israel, Its Life and Culture* (trans. by A. Møller and A. I. Fausbøll), 4 vols. in 2, London, 1926-40, III-IV, pp. 1-8.

41. Contrast, however, the analysis of O. Grether, *Das Deboralied. Eine metrische Rekonstruktion*, Gütersloh, 1941 (Beitr. z. Förderung Christl. Theol. Bd. 43, Heft 2). This book was not available to the writers, but a summary of its contents was supplied by Prof. Albright. Cf. also W. Rudolph, "Textkritische Anmerkungen zum Richterbuch", *Festschrift Otto Eissfeldt zum 60. Geburtstag* 1. September 1947 (ed. J. Fück), Halle, 1947, pp. 199-212.

42. See the detailed treatment of the Song of Miriam in Chapter II.

43. Cp. the discussion and study of the Song of Miriam by Haupt, "Moses' Song of Triumph", pp. 149-172. His reconstruction is too rigid, eliminating all the bicola 3:3.

44. These occur in vss. 5, 8b, 11a, 14, 16b.

45. These occur in vss. 1, 6, 10, 11b-12, 13, 16a.

46. These occur in vss. 3-4, 7-8a, 9, 15, 17.

47. These features confirm the antiphonal character of the poem, already so described in the Massoretic text. They suggest a three-part division of musical roles. Actual presentation of the song may have involved a much more complex choral fusion of the parts, impossible to indicate in a written text.

48. Cf. Albright, "The Earliest Forms of Hebrew Verse", pp. 84-86. The basic pattern is unquestionably correct, though in detail the reconstruction may be too rigidly conceived.

49. Cf. Albright, "The Old Testament and Canaanite Language", pp. 22f.; also Chapter IV, note 16.

50. Cf. Chapter IV, note 55, תבא or תהי.

51. Cf. Chapter III, note 84, תהין.

52. Cf. Albright, "The Psalm of Habakkuk", footnote k.

53. Albright, "The Oracles of Balaam", p. 212, note 23.

54. Chapter III, note 67, יגדנ (Gen. 49:19); note 84, תהין (Gen. 49:26).

55. Song of Deborah, footnote q, תשלחנ (Jud. 5:26); also footnote j, תדרכנ.

56. Chapter IV, note 25, תבאן (Deut. 33:7).

57. This form was apparently much more common in old poetry, to judge from the frequent preservation of the longer form in the Maccabaean Isaiah ms.

58. Chapter IV, note 16.

59. See especially Albright, "The Oracles of Balaam", p. 215, note 48, and p. 216, note 54; also references in Chapter IV, note 53. Other instances are common throughout the corpus.

60. For discussion, see Chapter II, note 19.

61. Cf. Albright, "The Oracles of Balaam", p. 215, note 48; p. 212, note 16.

62. The longer forms are preserved regularly in the first Isaiah ms., in accordance with a standardizing process exactly the reverse of that employed in the consonantal Massoretic text, where the shorter forms are regularly used.

63. Cf. Albright, "The Oracles of Balaam", p. 210.

64. Cf. Gordon, *Ugaritic Handbook*, I, 10:5.

65. Cf. Chapter V, notes 20, 35, 42; also Patton, *Canaanite Parallels in the Book of Psalms*, p. 34 for other references.

66. Cf. Gordon, *Ugaritic Handbook*, I, 12:6.

67. Chapter IV, note 62.

68. Cf. Chapter IV, note 8; Chapter V, note 41; Albright, "The Oracles of Balaam", p. 219, note 83.

69. See Albright's discussion of this phenomenon in "The Oracles of Balaam", p. 219, note 83.

70. Cf. Chapter II, notes 34 and 35.

71. Cf. Albright, "The Oracles of Balaam", p. 216, note 56.

72. This term is perhaps more suitable to the form in question. The term "omnitemporal" implies that the *yqtl* may have past or future significance in all cases, whereas in any particular case it may have any one time aspect, but only one.

73. See Chapter V, introduction, and the notes on the verses mentioned in the main part of the chapter.

74. The use of the conjunction is very rare in Ugaritic, and in the Massoretic text of considerable portions of the corpus of ancient Israelite poetry. There is thus excellent reason to believe that the same canon applied to old Hebrew poetry as to Ugaritic.

75. See the treatment in Chapter V of the use of the conjunction in these texts, and its bearing upon this matter. Note also the parallel texts Gen. 49:25-26 = Deut. 33:13-16. The conjunction is used regularly in the passage in Deut. 33, while it is lacking in Gen. 49, which preserves the more original form of the blessing in this respect.

76. In Ex. 15, the conjunction hardly appears at all. At the same time, the alternation of *qtl* and *yqtl* forms is common.

77. The material for this section is drawn largely from its companion work, *Early Hebrew Orthography*, AOS 36, New Haven: American Oriental Society, 1952.

78. In difficult and corrupt passages, the tendency would be for the scribe simply to copy the text as it stood. If he did not understand the meaning of the passage, he would be unable to revise the orthography in accordance with the practice current in his own day. The great bulk of archaic spellings inevitably crop up in such passages. See further discussion below.

79. On the date and interpretation of the Gezer Calendar, see Albright, "The Gezer Calendar", *BASOR* #92 (1943), pp. 16-26.

80. *Ibid.*, pp. 22ff.

81. Cf. Albright, "The Phoenician Inscriptions of the Tenth Century B.C. from Byblus", *JAOS* 67 (1947), pp. 153-160.

82. This usage may have been introduced under the influence of Aramaic orthographic practice. In Aramaic, *aleph* ultimately replaced *he* as the sign for final *â*. In Arabic the later Aramaic system was adopted, and the use of *aleph* extended so that it represents long *a* in all positions. The use of *aleph* as a *mater lectionis* in Hebrew was always much more limited, and it never displaced *he*.

83. *The Evolution of Early Hebrew Orthography*, p. 211, note 27.

84. We adopt a Maccabaean date for the first Isaiah scroll, following Drs. Albright, Birnbaum, Ginsberg, Sukenik, and the great majority of scholars.

85. According to latest reports, one of the mss. in the possession of the Hebrew University is a second copy of the Book of Isaiah (not complete). The orthography of this ms. corresponds much more closely to that of the Massoretic text than that of the first Isaiah scroll. We are indebted to Prof. Albright for this information.

86. By the time of the Massoretes, the consonantal text was fixed. Revision was therefore limited to vocalization by the use of vowel points.

87. A number of "archaic" spellings result from scribal attempts to restore the standard text, in which, by regularly substituting a short spelling for the longer one, pseudo-archaisms appear. An example of this is the second masculine singular pronominal suffix, as it appears in MT. Originally this was *-kā̆*, written in the early stage of Hebrew orthography simply ך. In due course, the final vowel was dropped in colloquial speech, producing the form *-ak*; the longer form was preserved in the literary language. After the introduction of final vowel letters, the long form would have been written כה, and the short form ך. In the first Isaiah scroll, the longer form regularly appears, indicating a pronunciation *-kā*. In the more conservative orthography of the second Isaiah scroll, the short form would be regular ך, following the orthography of the Lachish Letters and presumably, older Hebrew mss. The Massoretes substituted the literary form for the colloquial form, and pointed the final *kaph*, ךָ. Superficially, the final result is identical

with the early tenth century orthography of the second person suffix. Actually, it is a pseudo-archaism, the result of a long and complex history of transmission, involving linguistic change and orthographic revision and standardization.

88. Cf. footnote 78.

CHAPTER II

THE SONG OF MIRIAM

CHAPTER II

THE SONG OF MIRIAM

It seems fitting to designate the hymn in Exodus 15, "The Song of Miriam". Such a title need imply nothing as to the authorship of the poem. It does, however, distinguish the poem from the "Song of Moses" in Deut. 32, and suggests the superiority of the tradition (E?) which associates the song with Miriam rather than with Moses. It is easy to understand the ascription of the hymn to the great leader. It would be more difficult to explain the association of Miriam with the song as a secondary development. Moreover, the designation indicates with regard to the nature and structure of the poem, that it is an occasional piece, with a unified pattern including vss. 1b - 18. The opening verse also served as the title of the song in antiquity, in accordance with standard practice in entitling poems. Hence vs. 21 is not a different or shorter or the original version of the song, but simply the title of the song, taken from a different cycle of traditions.

No thoroughgoing study of the poem has been made since Canaanite poetic materials have become generally available. For example, one of the latest treatments, that of Beer in 1939[a], shows no acquaintance with the new extra-biblical materials, nor the bearing of the latter on linguistic studies and our understanding of early Hebrew prosody.

As indicated in the introduction, the Song of Miriam is a song of triumph and in this respect is to be closely associated with the Song of Deborah. Such scholars as Haupt[b], Mowinckel[c], Schmidt[d] and Beer[e] may well be right in supposing that the poem was used liturgically on festal occasions.[f] In fact, the excellent state of the text suggests that the song was very popular throughout Israelite history. It is to be emphasized, however, that the poem does not find its *origin* in the late cultus, and that vs. 1b cannot be split off from the rest of the song, the latter part then being classified as a hymn of praise which was inserted into the JE or JEP complex at a later date.[g]

In its metrical style and strophic structure, the poem fits precisely into the pattern of old Canaanite and early Hebrew poetry. The repetitive parallelism, mixed meter, and the complex makeup of the strophes, suggest an early date of composition. At the same time, the unity of the pattern and the symmetry of the strophic structure[h] indicate that the poem is substantially a single, unified composition.[i] Insertions or expansions would certainly mar the meter and strophic pattern.[j]

Older critical scholarship was rather disposed to date a considerable part of the song in the period of the united kingdom, or even earlier. It was also observed that the song is clearly independent of the JE and P accounts of the crossing of the Reed Sea.[k] More recent commentators, assuming a late date for the song, argue that it is dependent upon the account in JE(P).[l] Scholars pressing for a late date, note that the song is vague with regard to the miraculous events, and assert therefore that it must be further removed from the historical scene! Others contend that because the JE and P narratives are not verbally dependent upon the song, therefore it is probably later than the narratives. The reverse is equally plausible, however, since the song is not dependent upon the JE or P accounts. Actually, if the poem is substantially a unit, which is the contention of this study, inserted into the narrative of one tradition (J?), and if vs. 21 is the title of the song, mentioned in the narrative of the other tradition (E?), then it would appear that the poem were prior to the written composition of either, and that both J and E had knowledge of the ancient victory hymn.[m]

Since the appearance of Bender's influential article on the language of Exodus 15[n], scholars have made much of alleged Aramaisms in the song, and its "archaizing" style.[o] Recent advances in our knowledge of the historical grammar and lexicography of Hebrew have changed the picture completely. Much of the evidence of supposedly "late" language and style actually points to an early date. For details see the notes to the Hebrew text. The poem is not archaizing, but archaic.

The relationship between the content of the song and that of the prose narratives, J and P[p], is a matter of some dispute. The poem itself, if read with an appreciation of hyperbolic Semitic imagery and figurative language, tells no explicit narrative. So far as the action is concerned, it describes only the destruction of the Egyptians, with an allusion to the safe transit of the Israelites. Nothing is related, however, of the manner of the Israelite crossing. Vs. 8 and 10 describe in highly colored terms the wind and waves of a tempest at sea. The Egyptians were drowned in a storm sent by Yahweh. The Egyptians were hurled into the sea (vs. 1b, 4), and sank under the waters (vs. 5, 10). It is a mistake to see in the phrases, "the waters are heaped up" and "the swells mount as a wall" (vs. 8), a description of a path miraculously appearing between two walls of water; though it is not difficult to regard the P account of the episode as being based upon a literalistic interpretation of the poetic phrases. The J story is more in accord with the poem, though even here differences are noteworthy. In J, the wind drives the waters back for the benefit of the Israelites (Ex. 14:21b), while in the poem, it is the source of a sudden squall which overturns the vessels or barges upon which the Egyptian host had embarked.[q]

It would appear, therefore, that the Song of Miriam is the oldest of the extant sources for this event in Israelite history, being earlier than the parallel prose narratives just as the Song of Deborah is clearly anterior to the prose account in Judges 4. The priority of the poetic form of the tradition over the prose form is normally to be expected in this cultural milieu.

It does not seem possible to date the poem precisely. In addition to the evidence presented above, the orthographic data, linguistic characteristics, and metrical structure point to a *terminus ad quem* in the tenth century for its written composition. This suggests a date in the period of the Judges for its oral composition. Vs. 17 is no longer useful for dating purpose (see footnote 56 of this chapter), nor is vs. 18 (see footnote 59). The list of nations in vs. 14-15, along with the omission of the Ammonites (see footnote 42), may mean that the poem in substantially its present form was in circulation as early as the twelfth century B.C. The poem is roughly contemporaneous with the Oracles of Balaam and the Song of Deborah, and may be the earliest of the three.

In the following study of the text of the poem, we have made extensive use of the unpublished notes of Professor Albright, which he kindly placed at our disposal.

Notes to the Introduction

a. G. Beer, *Exodus mit einem Beitrag von K. Galling (Handbuch zum A. T., 1,3)*, Tübingen, 1939, pp. 79-84.

b. P. Haupt, "Moses' Song of Triumph", *AJSL* XX (1904), pp. 149-172, esp. p. 152.

c. S. Mowinckel, *Psalmenstudien II: Das Thronbesteigungsfest Jahwäs und der Ursprung der Eschatologie* (*Videnskapsselskapets Skrifter*, II, Hist.-Filos. Klasse, 1921, No. 6), Kristiania, 1922, *passim*, esp. pp. 56, 111f.

d. H. Schmidt, "Das Meerlied, Ex 15:2-19", *ZAW* 49 (NF 8), (1931), pp. 59-66, esp. p. 66.

e. Beer, *Exodus*, p. 84.

f. It seems quite probable that the poem was recited on such occasions as the Passover, and accompanied by dancing as suggested by tradition (vs. 21).

g. So also Mowinckel, *Psalmenstudien II*, pp. 111, note 4.

h. Analysis of the poem reveals a mixed meter, and an alternation of theme and counter-theme or refrain in the structure of the strophes. This points to the antiphonal character of the song; it is hazardous to venture beyond this. Schmidt's elaborate arrangement of the material according to voices and choirs is highly subjective. We can only guess at some of the possible ways in which the victory ode was presented by bards, or in the cultus.

i. For a review of the metrical and strophic analyses of various scholars, cf. Haupt, "Moses' Song of Triumph", pp. 150ff.; also Schmidt, "Das Meerlied, Ex 15:2-19", pp. 59ff.

j. For a possible instance of this, see the discussion of Ex. 15:2 in note 3 of this chapter.

k. Cf. S. R. Driver (following Dillmann), *The Book of Exodus* (*The Cambridge Bible for Schools and Colleges*), Cambridge, 1911, p. 124.

l. Cf. Haupt, "Moses' Song of Triumph", p. 154; and A. H. McNeile, *The Book of Exodus* (*Westminster Commentaries*) 2nd ed., London, 1917, p. 88.

m. For reminiscences of the Song of Miriam in late biblical literature, see Driver's collection in *The Book of Exodus*, p. 131.

n. A. Bender, "Das Lied Exodus 15", *ZAW* 23 (1903), pp. 1-48.

o. Haupt, in fairness, refutes the contention that Aramaisms exist in the text, despite the fact that he regards Bender's date for the poem (450 B.C.) as too high!

p. E material is elusive in this section, and cannot be isolated in a satisfactory manner.

q. For the latest discussion of the route and historical circumstances of the Exodus utilizing recent archaeological evidence, see W. F. Albright, "Exploring in Sinai with the University of California African Expedition", *BASOR* #109 (1948), pp. 5-20, esp. pp. 15f.

The Song of Miriam

I:1

Let me sing to Yahweh	(1)	אשר[1] ליהו	2	
For he is highly exalted		כ גא גא	2	
Horse and chariotry		סס ורכב[2]	2	
He hath cast into the sea		רמ בים [][3]	2	

Yahweh is a warrior	(3)	יהו <גבר>[4] []	2	
Yahweh is his name		יהו שמ	2	
{The chariots of Pharaoh} {Pharaoh and his army}	(4)	[5]{מרכבת פרע[6]} {⸢פרע⸣ וחל}	2	
He hath hurled into the sea.		יר בים	2	
His chosen troops		[7]⸢מבחר שלשר[8]	2	
Are drowned in the Reed Sea.		טבע[9] בים סף	2	

The deeps covered them	(5)	תהמת יכסים[10]----[11]	3	
..... They sank in the depths like a stone.		ירד במצלת[12] כמ-אבן	3	

I:2

Thy right hand, Yahweh	(6)	ימנכ[13] יהו	2	AB
Who art fearful in power		נאדכ[14] בכח	2	CD
Thy right hand, Yahweh		ימנכ יהו	2	AB
Shatters the enemy		תרעץ איב	2	EF

In thy great majesty	(7)	[15]ברב גאנכ[16]	2
Thou dost smash thine adversaries		תהרס קמכ[17]	2
Thou dost send forth thy fury		תשלח חרנכ	2
It consumes them like stubble		יאכלמ[18] כקש	2
At the blast of thy nostrils	(8)	[19]ברח אפכ[20]	2
The waters are heaped up.		נערמ מם	2

The swells mount as a wall		נצב כמ-נד[21] נזלמ[22]	3
The deeps churn in the midst of the sea.		קפא[23] תהמת בלב ים	3

I:3

Said the enemy	(9)	[24]אמר איב	2
I will give chase, I will overtake		ארדף אשג	2
I will divide spoil		אחלק שלל	2
My greed will be sated		תמלאמ[25] נפש	2
I will bare my sword		ארק חרב	2
My hand will conquer.		תרשמ[26] יד	2

Thou didst blow with thy breath	(10)	נשמת ברחכ	2
The sea covered them		כסמ[27] ים	2
They sank like a lead weight		צלל[28] כעפרת	2
Beneath the dreadful waters.		במם אדרמ[29]	2

Who is like thee among the mighty ones, Yahweh?	(11)	מ[30]-[31]כמכ[32] באלמ[33] יהו	3
Who is like thee feared among the holy ones?		מ-כמכ נאדר[34] בקדש<מ>[35]	3

The One who is revered for laudable acts		נרא תהלת[36]	2
The One who performs wondrous deeds		עש פלא[37]	2
Thou didst stretch out thy right hand	(12)	נטת ימנכ	2
The earth swallowed them.		תבלעמ ארץ	2

II:1

Thou didst faithfully lead	(13)	נחת בחסדכ	2
The people whom thou didst deliver		עם [38]ז-גאלת	2
Thou didst guide in thy might		נהלת[39] בעזכ	2
To thy holy encampment.		אל נו[40] קדשכ	2

The peoples heard, they shuddered	(14)	שמע עממ ירגזן[41]	3
Horror seized the dwellers of Philistia.		חל אחז ישב פלשת[42]	3

Yea, they were dismayed	(15)	אז[43] נבהל	2
The chieftains of Edom		אלפ אדם	2
The nobles of Moab		אל[44] מאב	2
Were seized with trembling		יאחזמ רעד[45]	2
They were utterly terrified		נמג כל[46]	2 } 3(?)
The dwellers of Canaan		ישב כנען	2 }

Thou hast brought down on them	(16)	חפל[47] עלהם	2
Terror and dread		אמת[48] ופחד	2
By thy sovereign might		בגדל[49] זרעכ	2
They are struck dumb like a stone.		ידמ[50] כאבן	2

II:2

When thy people passed over, Yahweh		עד-יעבר[51] עמכ יהו	3
When thy people passed over, whom thou hast created.		עד-יעבר עמ<כ>[52] ז-[53]קנת[54]	3

Thou didst bring them, Thou didst plant them	(17)	תבאמ [55]י⌝תטעמ	2
In the mount of thy heritage.		בהר[56] נחלתכ	2
The dais of thy throne		מכן לשבתכ	2
Thou hast made, Yahweh		פעלת[57] יהו	2
A sanctuary, Yahweh,		מקדש <יהו>[58]	2
Thy hands established.		כננ ידכ	2

Yahweh reigns	(18)	יהו ימלך[59]	2
Forever and ever!		לעלם ועד	2

Notes to the Text

1. Massoretic *'āšîrâ* is suitable. Textual evidence, however, shows that we are dealing, in this verse, with variant readings of great antiquity. The parallel in vs. 21 reads *šîrû* which is perhaps metrically more exact. On the other hand, the Hebrew underlying the LXX, Peshitta, and Vulgate, seems to have been *nāšîrâ*, which harmonizes well with the introduction to the song. The Samaritan reads אשרו, apparently a conflate text, combining *'āšîrâ* and *šîrû*. The use of the first person in victory odes is quite proper, however, cf. Jud. 5:3. Similar variations in the opening lines of a hymn are to be found in Num. 10:35 // Ps. 68:2, etc.

2. MT is awkward; LXX (αναβάτην), Vulgate, Old Latin and Syro-hexaplar presuppose *rôkēb*, which is scarcely an improvement. Haupt, "Moses' Song of Triumph', *ad loc.*, suggests *rékeb*, and observes that ἅρμα is found in the margin of one Greek ms. Cp. also *rikbô* in vs. 19. The final vowel letter (*waw*) would not have appeared in the early orthography. It is to be noted that the verse scans more easily if case endings are retained. From an historical point of view, רכבו must be interpreted as referring to chariotry, or conceivably to the charioteers. There is now excellent evidence that cavalry were not introduced into the Near East until the late twelfth century B.C., and probably not into Egypt until considerably later. Israel does not seem to have made use of cavalry until some time in the ninth century, cf. Albright, *Archaeology and the Religion of Israel*, 2nd ed., Baltimore, 1946, p. 213, note 25.

3. Vs. 2 which appears to be a couplet, 3:3.3:3, does not conform to the metrical structure which prevails throughout the remainder of the song. It also seems to be out of context at this point in the poem. The first bicolon is a common ascription of praise, found again in Isa. 12:2b and Ps. 118:14. It may have been used here as an introductory doxology, before the body of the poem, beginning at vs. 3 (vs. 1b being taken as a refrain). The antiquity of the couplet is not at all affected by these considerations, as the following notes will indicate:

My might and my defense are Yahweh	(2)	עז[a] וזמרת[b] יה⌈ו⌉[c]
And he hath saved me		יהי לי[d] לישע
This is my God whom I exalt		ז אל ⌈אכממנה⌉[e]
The God of my father whom I admire		אלה אב[f] ⌈אנוה⌉

a. The LXX and Peshitta read simply עז. MT (followed by the Vulgate) is doubtless correct. The versions, however, give evidence of the early phonetic orthography in Israel. See note b.

b. Read *zimrātî*, supported by the Samaritan and the Vulgate. The *mater lectionis*, *yodh*, seems not to have been read by the mass of Massoretic texts, along with the LXX (βοηθός), and the Peshitta. It is possible that these latter witnesses preserve early orthography; or a simple haplography of *yodh* may be involved. The meaning "protection, defense", is supported by the South Arabic, Arabic (?), and North Israelite (cf. Samaria Ostraca #12 ll. 1,2,3), and Aramaic proper names. Cf. T.H. Gaster, "Notes on 'the Song of the Sea'", *Expository Times* 48 (1936-37), p. 45, for discussion. For another occurrence of זמרת with this meaning, cf. II Sam. 23:1, "The anointed of the God of Jacob and the favorite of the 'Defense' of Israel."

c. The complex יהויהי is best divided and read as follows: *yahwê yihyê*. Yahweh in early orthography would have been written simply יהו. For the latest treatment of the morphology of the tetragrammaton, cf. Albright, *JBL* LXVII (1948), pp. 379-380. The defective orthography in the case of *yihyê* is also an example of early spelling.

d. On the orthography of this word, see Albright, "The Oracles of Balaam", p. 212, note 16.

e. As MT stands, the second colon is considerably longer than the first. The simplest solution to this metrical imbalance is to interchange the verbs; this produces the desired symmetry. The transposition of words is not an uncommon phenomenon in the transmission of a text, especially in a case where both words begin and end with the same letters. It can now be illustrated by comparison of the new Isaiah scroll with the MT. Cf. Burrows, "Variant Readings in the Isaiah Manuscript", *BASOR* #111 (1948), pp. 23, 24.

Prof. Albright associates אנוהו (cf. Hab. 2:5 ינוה) with Arab. *nwy*, Ethiopic *newa*, Ugar. *nwyt*, "settlement", Hebrew *nawê*, "pastoral or nomadic abode", *nawâ*, "range, pasture"; etc. He derives these from a root meaning, "to aim at", which then develops in two directions: "to look or gaze ardently at", and "to reach or settle". The Hiphil here may be translated, "I will make him a cynosure, I will admire him (i.e., I will cause him to be the object of ardent gazing)." The versions interpret the word correctly, either from knowledge of its true meaning, or from context.

The preservation of the energic *nun* in וארממנה is archaic. Cf. Deut. 32:10 bis; and in later archaizing poetry, Ps. 72:15 and Jer. 5:22.

f. It is difficult to determine whether *'ābî* would appear in early orthography as אב or אבי. The first person singular pronominal suffix attached to a genitive noun of this type is regularly indicated by a *yodh* in the orthography of early Phoenician inscriptions. The differentiation of such pronominal forms attached to nouns in the genitive case is already found in Ugaritic; cf. Gordon, *Ugaritic Handbook*, I 6:16, and Z. Harris, *A Grammar of the Phoenician Language*, New Haven, 1936, p. 48, where the occurrence of אב (nominative), "my father", and אבי (genitive), "my father", in the Kilamuwa inscription is discussed.

4. The Samaritan reads גבור במלחמה, followed in part by the LXX, συντρίβων πολέμους, and the Peshitta, ܓܢܒܪܐ ܘܡܩܪܒܬܢܐ. We suggest that there were two ancient variants: *yahwê gibbôr*, and (*yahwê*) *'îš milḥāmâ* (cf. Haupt, "Moses' Song of Triumph", *ad loc.*). One variant is represented by MT, while the texts quoted above represent more or less corrupt conflations of the two readings. For metrical reasons, *gibbôr* seems the preferable reading. Note the archaic poetic structure, ab:ac, also found in the Song of Deborah, Jud. 5:3. Cp. Ps. 24:8, Ezek. 39:20, and the difficult passage in Ps. 68:5.

5. The first colon is hypermetrical. Prof. Albright suggests that מרכבת פרעה and פרעה וחלו are ancient variants.

6. The final *he* in *parᶜô* is a vowel letter. *He* was introduced after the tenth century to represent all final vowels except *î* and *û*. Probably it arose as a *mater lectionis* for final

â, the two sounds being most nearly homogeneous, just like *waw* = *û*, and *yodh* = *î*, which were also introduced about the same time. The use of *he* in this manner may be traced to cases in which final consonantal *he* followed *a*, such as forms with the feminine suffix, words with *he* directive (the *he* was originally consonantal as shown by Ugaritic), true *lamedh-he* verbs, forms like the interrogative *mâ* (Ugar. *mh*), etc. Not infrequently in this situation, -*āh*, the *he* quiesces; and if retained in the spelling, it becomes automatically a *mater lectionis* for final *â*. This use of *h*- was then extended to all cases of final *a*, and also to include the vowels *o* and *e*. This development, which is common to Aramaic and Hebrew orthography, is amply illustrated by numerous examples from the earliest Aramaic inscriptions, the Mesha Stone, and post-tenth century Hebrew inscriptions. The extension in the use of *he* to represent final *ô* and *ê* may easily have arisen in the so-called weak verbs, where the *mater lectionis he* is used as a substitute for the lost consonant in all forms (e.g. *gālâ*, *yiglê*, *g*^{e}*lê*, *gālô*, etc.). As a *mater lectionis* for final *ô*, *he* was in general use in the ninth-seventh centuries (e.g., נבה, "Nebo", Mesha Stone, line 14), though it was in part replaced by *waw* after the Exile. Survivals of such orthography in the Bible may be seen in the following examples: שלמה, "Solomon"; שוכה "Socoh" (so spelled occasionally in the Massora, cf. Ginsberg, "MMṢT and MṢH", *BASOR* #109 [1948], pp. 20f.); שלה, "Shiloh"; ירחה, "Jericho"; גלה, "Giloh"; and the particles פה, "here", כה, "thus"; etc. Such historical spelling is preserved in the biblical text primarily in proper names, *lamedh-he* verbs, and special words. The third person masculine singular suffix (-*ô*) was represented by the vowel letter *he* as shown by the Siloam Inscription, the Lachish Letters and other inscriptional data, as well as survivals in MT (see GK §91e). The *he* in this instance has commonly been regarded as the survival of an historical spelling for older -*ahû* > -*aw* > -*ô*. Such a view now seems unlikely, since it appears that for a considerable time after -*ahû* had become *ô*, the consonantal *he* having been lost, it was replaced by zero in the orthography. For this reason, the later general use of *he* in the final position for *â* and *ê*, as well as *ô*, seems unrelated to its earlier use in the suffix form. For an extended discussion of this matter, cf. *Early Hebrew Orthography, passim.*

7. Omit the *waw* with the LXX and Vulgate. See the study of the conjunction introducing cola in Chapter V.

8. On שלשו, Ugar. *ṯlṯ* see Y. Sukenik, "Note on *ṯlṯ swsm* in the Legend of Keret", *JCS* II (1948), pp. 11-12.

9. MT *ṭubb*^{ec}*û* may be correct. The Peshitta (ܛܒܥ) and important witnesses of the LXX (AF) seem to have read **ṭibba*^{c}, "he drowned (them)". Either reading makes acceptable sense. Since in early orthography, the word would have been written without the final *waw*, both interpretations were possible from the earliest times.

10. This form is doubly archaic, preserving the final *yodh* of the root (cf. Albright, "The Phoenician Inscriptions of the Tenth Century B.C. from Byblus", *JAOS* 67 [1947], p. 154), as well as the archaic suffix (*-mû* = *-mô*). Scholars have often commented upon the consistent use of *-mô* in Ex. 15 as the third masculine plural pronominal suffix (cf. GK §91:L3). This has been explained as an instance of conscious archaizing, but it is at least as reasonable to suppose that genuinely archaic forms have survived. Archaizing is generally characterized by the misuse or mixed use of ancient forms, not by consistently correct use. The latter phenomenon points rather to the antiquity of the poem. It is further objected that the suffix in Ex. 15 occurs only with verbs, and is therefore suspect, presumably because we would expect to find it with nouns also (cf. GK §91:L3). Such an argument readily is answered by the fact that no nouns appear in the poem with the third masculine plural suffix. A single form (^{ca}*lêhem*, vs. 16) deviates from the consistent use of the *-mô* suffix in the poem, and we may have here a survival of a still older form of the suffix from which both *-hem* and *-mô* are derived (cf. footnote 48).

11. Metrical analysis shows that one stress has dropped out of the text. Something like *b*^{e}*yām* (vss. 1, 4) or *b*^{e}*lēb yām* (vs. 8) would be expected. Either of these might have fallen out by homoioteleuton (in the old orthography, the previous word would have appeared as יכסימ).

12. See footnote 28 on *ṣāl*^{e}*lû*.

13. Note the archaic repetition (cf. vs. 3, footnote 4). This is a variation of the well-known pattern, abc:abd, to conform to the 2:2 metrical structure.

14. In *ne'dārî*, we have a recognized instance of the preservation of the old genitive case ending, at a time when case endings were largely confused or lost. For the syntax, cf. GK §130a. The versions translate the phrase *ne'dārî bakkoaḥ* as referring to *yemînekā* rather than to *yahwê*. This is, of course, syntactically incorrect if they read MT. It does not seem that they used a different Hebrew text, but rather represent a questionable interpretation of the received text. From the point of view of poetic symmetry, it may be a preferable reading. To emend the text from *ne'dārî* to **ne'dārâ* or **ne'dārat* seems unnecessary, however, since MT makes acceptable sense. On the other hand, the influence of *ne'dār baqqōdeš* in vs. 11 may have affected the reading here.

The term *ne'dārî* is best interpreted in its archaic sense here, "the One-to-be-feared", i.e., "the Awesome One" (cp. Ugar. *'adr*, 2D VI:20-23; Acc. *adâru*, "to fear", etc.). The word *'addîr* in Hebrew later developed the meaning, "majestic one" or "glorious one".

15. Omit the *waw* with the Peshitta, and for stylistic reasons. Cf. note 24.

16. Cp. the use of *ga'ān* in Ugaritic, II D:VI:43,4.

17. This is a frequently used word in archaic poetry, cf. Deut. 32:25, 33:11; II Sam. 22:40,49 = Ps. 18:40,49; Ugar. 76: II:24, etc.

18. On the archaic suffix, see note 10.

19. Omit the *waw* with the Peshitta, and for stylistic reasons. See note 24.

20. *berûaḥ 'appêkā* refers to the wind as the breath of Yahweh's nostrils; cf. II Sam. 22:16 = Ps. 18:16.

21. This is a rare word, apparently meaning hill or heap. The other occurrences of the word are related to this passage, and are probably dependent upon it. Cf. Josh. 3:13,16; Ps. 78:13. The other occurrences are obscure and perhaps corrupt.

22. Cf. Num. 24:7, Deut. 32:2, and Jud. 5:5(?) for the use of this term in ancient contexts.

23. The meaning of the verb is difficult to determine. Apparently the translators also had difficulty. The LXX renders ἐπάγη, the same word used to translate *niṣṣebû*. The Vulgate reads *congregatae sunt*, the same form which is used to render *necermû*. The Peshitta uses a cognate word, which provides strong

support for the received text. The principal meaning of the word so far as it may be interpreted from other Old Testament contexts, seems to be "congeal" or "coagulate". We may suppose an earlier meaning "churn", "ferment" or "work" from which the later meanings were derived. With respect to milk, "to churn" and "to coagulate" or in the case of wine, "to ferment" and "to thicken" are not long jumps in thought. In the present context, the former idea, involving action, is preferable.

24. Note the staccato style; cp. Jud. 5:25,26. It is also common in Ugaritic literature. Omission of the conjunction is to be considered a stylistic characteristic of early poetry. In the transmission of the text, however, there was a tendency to introduce the conjunction at the beginning of cola. The secondary character of these conjunctions is indicated by the comparison of parallel texts such as II Sam. 22 and Psalm 18 (see Chapter V), cf. Chapter IV, note 3. Comparison with the Peshitta of this passage will illustrate the tendency to insert the conjunction into the text. A similar passage is to be found in II Sam. 22:38-39 (Ps. 18:38-39), where the staccato style has been obscured in part. The alliteration in this verse is perhaps deliberate.

25. Read *timlā'ēm*, as suggested to the writers by Prof. Albright; the suffix does not belong here, and the *mem* clearly is enclitic. The verse may be translated: "My soul will be filled (sated)..." The Vulgate interprets the colon in precisely this way; the LXX seems to read another form of the verb, but without the suffix (ἐμπλήσω). In early orthography, the word, with or without the suffix, would have been written simply with final *mem*. In certain texts, the enclitic *mem* survived, and was later interpreted as a sign of the suffix. The addition of the vowel letter produced the present MT. In other texts, the archaic *mem* was dropped, and this resulted in the text underlying the Vulgate (and LXX). The context and parallelism with the preceding cola strongly suggest that the suffix is not original here.

26. Read *tôrîšēm*, following Albright's suggestion. The *mem* is enclitic, as in *timlā'ēm*, cf. note 25. The LXX does not have the suffix here.

27. On the archaic form of the suffix, cf. note 10.

28. This word is a *hapax legomenon*. Etymologically it is connected with Acc. *ṣalâlu*, "sink, sink down", hence, "sleep", often of death. Further than that, the etymology is not clear. Two derivations are possible. The usual connection is with Aram. *ṣll*, "filter", and Arab. *ṣll*, "to strain, clarify". Perhaps better is the connection with So. Arab. 11B, "perish", Arab. *ḍll*, "perish, be absent", etc. The term *m*ᵉ*ṣûlâ*, "depth" may be related, "place of sinking(?)". In Ex. 15:5, it is parallel to *t*ᵉ*hōmôt*; in Ps. 68:23, with *bāšān* (= Ugar. *baṯnu*).

29. Cf. note 14.

30. This verse retains the repetitive style commented upon in notes 4 and 13. The pattern here is, ab:cd.ab:d'c'.

31. On the orthography of *-mi*, see Albright, "The Oracles of Balaam", pp. 209-210.

32. כמכה preserves post-tenth century orthography but the more archaic pronunciation. The Samaritan gives the common orthography of still later times: כמוך. On the problem of the longer and shorter forms of the suffix, see Chapter I, Section 5; on the suffix *-k(ā)* in particular, see Chapter I, footnote 87.

33. Cp. Ps. 29:1, 89:7; Deut. 32:8(LXX). See also note 35.

34. The Samaritan reads *ne'dārî*, which is grammatically correct here. It may have influenced the reading in vs. 6, or it may be a reminiscence of the form there, cf. note 14.

35. Read *q*ᵉ*dōš(îm)*, with the LXX and Syro-hexaplar, (so Haupt, "Moses' Song of Triumph", *ad loc.*). This reading is strongly suggested by the parallel phrase. For verbal and literary parallels, see Chapter IV, notes 6, 7, 9 and 13.

36. Translate תהלת, "praiseworthy acts", following Haupt, "Moses' Song of Triumph", p. 161. Cp. Isa. 63:7, Pss. 66:5, 78:4, etc. Cf. also Holzinger, *Exodus* (*Kurzer Handcommentar z. A.T.*), Tübingen, 1900, and Driver, *The Book of Exodus*.

37. MT is probably correct (cp. Ps. 77:15 where the identical words occur). The Samaritan reads פלאה, to be vocalized *pil'â* or perhaps *p*ᵉ*lî'â* as in late Hebrew. The form is otherwise unknown in biblical Hebrew. The LXX, Vulgate, and Peshitta all translate the word as plural, which may mean that the underlying Hebrew text read the plural, *p*ᵉ*lā'îm* or *p*ᵉ*lā'ôt*. On the other hand, the versions often translate the word *péle'* as plural, though it is singular in form, so the basis for emendation is extremely weak. Cp., for example, the Greek of Pss. 77:15,

88:11,13, 78:12, where Hebrew *péle'*, is translated by θαυμάσια. In Ps. 77:12 and 89:6, the LXX also reads plural for the singular of MT, but a number of Hebrew mss. have the plural form. To read *p^e lā'îm*, as suggested by Prof. Albright, would aid the meter and afford better parallelism in structure.

38. The older relative. See note 53.

39. Some critics, following the Vulgate, read *nēháltô*, "thou didst guide it", (for older **nēhaltāhû*). This would be in accord with standard prose syntax. But the absence of the object in this poetry is not a serious difficulty. By regarding the couplet as a unit, with the second verb of motion resuming the action of the first part, and referring back to the same object, and then carrying the action further to its conclusion, the syntactical problems are obviated.

40. An archaic designation of the divine sanctuary. The term *nāwê* strongly reflects the desert origin of Yahwism. Cf. note 3e.

41. For lexicographical parallels, see Hab. 3:2,16; Pss. 18:8, 77:17.

42. In a presumed thirteenth century context, the word פלשת is an anachronism. Its use here fixes the twelfth century as the *terminus a quo* for the poem in its present form. The omission of the Ammonites in this catalogue of nations is equally significant, and points to a *terminus ad quem* for the bulk of the poem in the eleventh century.

43. Read probably *'āzê*, the North Israelite, contracted form of *'āzāy*. *'āzāy* occurs in Ps. 123:3,4,5. This reading would be preferable on the basis of meter (so Albright); in the early orthography, the final vowel would not be indicated. The particle *'āz(ê)* occurs regularly in archaic poetry, cf. Gen. 49:4; Jud. 5:8,11,13,19,22; Ps. 89:20. Cp. Ugar. *'idk*, "then, thereupon".

44. For the expression *'êlê mô'āb*, "rams of Moab", cp. KRT B:IV:6,7 *ṣḥ . sb^c(m) . ṯry* (7) *ṯmnym . (ẓb)yy*; on this see Ginsberg, *The Legend of King Keret* (*BASOR*, *Supplementary Series* Nos. 2-3), American Schools of Oriental Research, New Haven, 1946, who compares this passage with Isa. 14:9; Ezek. 17:13. Note also II Sam. 1:19. In the parallel expression, *'allūpê*, we have a play on words; or it may have designated the leaders of the herd, or referred to animals originally.

45. The use of the *casus pendens* and a resumptive pronoun, together with the passive verb in the first colon, suggest that the Massoretic pointing may be incorrect. Without changing the consonantal text it is possible to read: *'êlê mô'āb yē'āḥ^{a}zûm rā́^{c}ad*, "the leaders of Moab are seized (with) trembling". However, the interpretation of *rā́^{c}ad* as an adverbial accusative involves certain difficulties, though in early Hebrew as in Arabic, the accusative case ending would have clarified its relationship to the verb.

46. The context suggests, and the metrical pattern would seem to require an adverbial form here with the meaning, "completely, totally, utterly". We may read the accusative **kulla*, or an adverbial formation in *-am*; cp. Acc. *kalāma*, Ugar. *klm*. The reading *kullâm*, "all of them", is also possible.

47. Read probably *tappîl*, "thou hast brought down".

48. MT is anomalous. The Samaritan reads the normal form, אימה. If the verse is scanned with case endings, the anomalous form is explained and the meter improved: *tappil(u) ^{c}alê(hi)m(u)*: *'emata wa-paḥda*.

49. Read probably *b^{e}gṓdĕl z^{e}rō̄^{c}^{a}kā*, "in the greatness of thy strength". The use of the adjective as a *nomen regens* in a construct chain is rare and difficult, cf. GK §132c. For the idiom, cf. Ps. 79:11; Num. 14:19.

50. The phrase is to be read *yiddammû kā'ā́ben*, "they are struck dumb like a stone". The *niphal* is the preferred form, and only a slight change in vocalization is required. To read *yidmû* with the LXX ("to be like a stone"), is contrary to Hebrew usage: דמה is regularly followed by *l^e* or *'el*.

51. The poetic pattern here is abc:abd. Cf. notes 4,13,30.

52. Read *^{c}amm^{e}kā*, in parallel with the first colon, and following the LXX and Vulgate. The omission in MT is due perhaps to the influence of עם-זו in vs. 13. The situation is reversed in the LXX, where for vs. 13, the Hebrew underlying the Greek apparently had עמך-זו, under the influence of the readings in this verse.

53. Read *zû-qanîtā* as a single unit. Interesting parallels occur in the introductory formulae of the tenth century Byblian inscriptions, where ז as a relative is closely connected with the verb of the dependent clause through the omission of the word divider; cf. Friedrich, "Zur Einleitungsformel der ältesten

phönizischen Inschriften aus Byblos", *Mélanges Dussaud*, Paris, 1939, pp. 37-47.

54. Translate *qānîtā*, "thou hast created", as in Deut. 32:6. The meaning "create" for this root is now well established in Ugaritic and biblical Hebrew. For a recent discussion of the verb and its use in biblical passages, see Ginsberg, *The Legend of King Keret*, p. 36, and "The North-Canaanite Myth of Anath and Aqhat: II", *BASOR* #98 (1945), p. 22, note 68. Of particular interest are the following passages: Gen. 14:19,22 and 4:1; Deut. 32:6; and in Ugaritic, II AB III:26,30; IV AB III:6,7; KRT A:57.

55. The conjunction is to be omitted for stylistic reasons. The LXX is not clear, but seems to omit it as well. Cf. note 24.

56. Vs. 17, and in particular the phrases *har naḥ^{a}lāt^{e}kā* and *mākôn l^{e}šibt^{e}kā* have often been considered clear references to Mt. Zion (so Haupt, "Moses' Song of Triumph", p. 163; the majority of scholars, however, take the first phrase as a general term for Canaan, cf. Driver, *The Book of Exodus*, *ad loc.*), and the Temple of Solomon (if not of the Second Commonwealth). The latter phrase is found in Solomon's prayer at the dedication of the Temple (I Kings 8:13), a quotation from the ancient Book of Jashar (so the LXX and Vulgate). On the passage in I Kings, see the reconstruction by W. F. Albright in his paper on "The Psalm of Habakkuk". These phrases, however, are much older than the time of Solomon, and were current in Canaanite long before the Israelite conquest. The poems of Ras Shamrah, from the fourteenth century, supply striking parallels, cf. Albright, *JBL* LXVII (1948), p. 381, note 5; *Archaeology of Palestine* (*Pelican Series*), Middlesex, 1949, pp. 232-233. In V AB C:26f, we find: *btk . ḡry . 'el . ṣpn* (27) *bqdš . bḡr . nḥlty.*, "in the midst of my mount (who am) the god of Ṣapon, in the holy place, in the mount of my inheritance". The same formula occurs in V AB D:64. In V AB F:15,16, II AB VIII:12ff., and *I AB II:15,16, the expressions *arṣ . nḥlth* and *kś'u . ṯbth*, "land of his inheritance", and "dais of his throne", are set in parallel. This mountain imagery was naturally applicable to Baal, god of Ṣapon; but it was also appropriate for Yahweh, whose close association with mountains is attested in the earliest sources (cf. Jud. 5:4-5; Pss. 18:7-15; 68:7-9,15-17; Hab. 3:3-15; etc.). These expressions, then, could have been used by the Israelite poet at any time, and do not in themselves point to a Solomonic (much less

a post-Solomonic) date for the poem. Later, of course, the phrases in question would be connected with Zion and the Temple at Jerusalem; and this interpretation, read back into the ancient ode would give special weight to the words of vs. 17.

57. This verb is quite common in early Yahwistic poetry, though rare in later materials. Cf. Num. 23:23; Deut. 32:4,27, 33:11; Ps. 68:29, 77:13; Hab. 3:2.

58. Read *yahwê* with 86 mss. and the Samaritan.

59. The kingship of the gods is a common theme in early Mesopotamian and Canaanite epics. The common scholarly position that the concept of Yahweh as reigning or king is a relatively late development in Israelite thought seems untenable in the light of this, and is directly contradicted by the evidence of the early Israelite poems; cf. Num. 23:21; Deut. 33:5; Ps. 68:25; Ps. 24:9.

CHAPTER III

THE BLESSING OF JACOB

CHAPTER III

THE BLESSING OF JACOB

We take up a distinctly different genre of ancient Yahwistic poetry with the tribal blessings, the Blessing of Jacob and the Blessing of Moses. To the same genre belong the tribal references in Jud. 5:14-18 and Ps. 68:28.[a] The Blessings also have certain characteristics in common with the Oracles of Balaam, but there are also strong contrasts.[b]

It seems probable in the light of *gattungs- und überlieferungsgeschichtlich* studies that individual blessings rest on ancient tradition. They circulated in oral form as folk literature, finally being gathered into collections. Some blessings are composite, such as those of Judah (Gen. 49:8-12) and Levi (Deut. 33:8-11), made up of originally separate elements. These illustrate the way in which blessings were brought together. On the other hand, the tendency to chop up the blessings into a host of fragments is the result of overly atomistic analysis. The Blessing of Jacob consists of a nucleus of blessings consciously set in the mouth of the Patriarch, (e.g. Reuben, Judah), to which have been appended blessings drawn from other sources (e.g., the Joseph blessing which occurs in slightly altered form in the Blessing of Moses). We may assume that groups of blessings, ascribed to Jacob and Moses, and perhaps others, circulated orally in the period of the Judges.

After the earlier classical pieces, the Songs of Deborah and Miriam, the blessings in these two collections are disappointing as literature. They are practically folk poetry, and lack the varied meter and complex rhetorical style of the victory odes. They delight in plays on words, frequently use rhyme, and with certain notable exceptions are uninspired in content.

With our increasing knowledge of the amphictyonic organization of the tribes in the period of the Judges[c], the place of the collection of tribal blessings in the religious and political life of the people has become clear. One may be assured that such collections were framed in this period from various cycles of oral tradition. It is most unlikely that the blessings were artificially set in a framework after the "twelve"-tribe system had ceased to be a living organization.

No serious question has been raised by scholars as to the pre-monarchic date of the majority of the individual blessings in Gen. 49. The only exception worthy of comment is the blessing of Judah, Gen. 49:8-11. As will be pointed out in the study which follows, this blessing is composite: vss. 8, 9, and 11-12 are individual units of a most archaic type. The short enigmatic blessing, vs. 10, is usually referred to the Judahite monarchy, the earliest possibility being the reign of David. An allusion to David is possible; more probably we have here pre-Davidic material which came naturally to be associated with the great king, was interpreted and may have been slightly modified in the light of his career and achievements. This is speculative, however, and it is quite impossible to date the collection on the basis of a doubtful understanding of a corrupt text. Judahite hegemony in the south during the period of the Judges may be all that is implied. It may be remarked that certain blessings, e.g. Reuben, Simeon and Levi, etc., may go back to patriarchal traditions. It is best to date the collection in substantially its present form in the late period of the Judges. Orthographic and linguistic criteria support such a date.

Notes to the Introduction

a. Ps. 68:28 seems to be the title or opening line of a poem dealing with an assembly of the tribes. According to Prof. Albright, Ps. 68 is a catalogue of ancient hymns, listing more than thirty by title (= opening line or lines).

b. See the treatment of the form of the Blessing in Gunkel's *Genesis* (*Handkommentar zum Alten Testament*), Göttingen, 1902, pp. 418ff. In many respects, this commentary on the Blessing is the best.

c. See, for example, the excellent study by M. Noth, *Das System der Zwölf Stämme Israels*, Stuttgart, 1930.

The Blessing of Jacob

Gather yourselves that I may inform you,	1b	האספ ואגד לכם [][1]	3
Assemble together, O sons of Jacob,	2	הקבצ []בנ יעקב	3
Hearken unto Israel your father.		⌐שמע אל ישראל אבכם	3

Reuben

Reuben, my first-born	3	ראבן בכר	2
Thou art my strength		את[2] כח	2
The prime of my manhood		⌐[3]ראשת אנ	2
The best of my might.		[4][]יתר עז[5][6]	2
....	4	------	
....		------[7]	
For thou didst go up to my bed		כ עלת <על> [8]משכב[9][]	3
Yea, thou didst profane the couch of thy father.		אז חללת יצע[10] <אבכ>[11]	3

Simeon and Levi

Simeon and Levi are brethren	5	שמען ולו אחם[12]	3
Weapons of violence are their merchandise		כל חמס מכרת[]ם[13]	3
Into their council enter not, O my soul	6	בסדם אל תבא[14] נפש	3
In their assembly join not, O my heart.		בקהלם אל תחד[15] כבד[16]	3
In their anger, they slew a man		[17][]באפם הרג אש	3
Willfully they houghed a bull.		⌐[18]ברצנם עקר שר[19]	3
Cursed be their anger, for it is fierce	7	ארר אפם כ-עז	3
And their wrath, for it is harsh.		ועברתם כ קשת	3

I will divide them in Jacob,		[20]אחלקם ביעקב	
I will scatter them in Israel.		אפצם בישראל[21]	

Judah

Judah, my splendor art thou,	8	יהד ⌜הד⌝[22] את[23]	3
Thy hand is on the neck of thine enemies.		[24]ידכ בערפ איבכ	3
Judah, thy brothers shall praise thee		[25] ⌜יהד⌝ ידכ אחכ	3
The sons of thy father shall bow down to thee.		ישתחו לכ בנ אבכ[25a]	3

A lion's whelp is Judah	9	[26]גר ארי יהד	3
From the prey, my son, thou hast gone up.		[27]מטרפ בנ עלת	3
He crouches, he couches like a lion,		[28]כרע רבץ כארי	3
Like a lioness, who dares rouse him?		[29]⌜י⌝כלבא מ יקמנ[30]	3

There shall not fail a judge from Judah	10	לא יסר שפ⌜פ⌝ט[31] מיהד	3
Nor a commander from among his standards		ומחקק[32] מבנ[33] י⌜ד⌝גלו	3
....		----------	
....		34----------	
His ass is harnessed with its bridle(?)	11	אסר[35] לגפנ[36] ער[37]	3
The colt of his she-ass with its trappings(?)		[38]⌜י⌝לשרק[39] בנ[40] אתנ	3
He dyes with wine his garment		כבס בינ לבש	3
With the blood of grapes his mantle.		[41]⌜י⌝בדם ענבם סות[42]	3

Darker are his eyes than wine	12	הכלל[43] ענם מין	3
Whiter his teeth than milk.		לבן[44] שנם מחלב[45]	3

Zebulun

Zebulun:	13	זבלן[46]	
At the shore of the seas he settles,		לחף ימם [ישב	3
At its inlets, he encamps.		על מפרצו][47] ישכן	3
....		------[48]	
....		------[49]	

Issachar

Issachar is an ass	14	ישׂשכר חמר ---[50]	3
He couches among the rubbish piles		רבץ בן[51] ⌜ר⌝משפתם[52]	3
He sees for himself a resting-place which is good	15	⌜י⌝רא[53] מנח[54] כ טב	3
He beholds for himself a land which is pleasant		[55] ⌜ה⌝יבט⌝ ארצ[56] כ נעם	3
He bends his shoulder to bear burdens		[57]⌜ד⌝יט שכמ לסבל	3
And he has become a corvée slave.		ויה למס עבד[58]	3

Dan

Dan pleads the cause of his people,	16	דן ידן <דן>[59] עם	3
The tribes of Israel together.		כאהד שבט ישראל	3
Dan is a serpent on the road,	17	[60][]דן בחש על דרך	3
A venomous snake on the path		שפפן על ארח	
Who snaps at the heels of a horse,		הנשך עקב[61] סס	
So that its rider falls backward.		ויפל[62] רכב[63] אהר[64] [][65]	

English	Verse	Hebrew	Count
		Gad	
Gad is a band that raids	19	גד גדד[66] יגדנ[67]	3
And he raids from the rear.		והא יגד עקב⌜ם⌝[68]	3
		Asher	
As for Asher, {his food is rich} {his land is fertile}	20	⌜ר⌝[69]אשר {שמן לחמ / שמנ-ארצ}[70]	3
He produces royal delicacies.		[ ][71] יתן[72] מעדנ מלך	3
		Naphtali	
....	21	------	
....		------[73]	
		Joseph	
....	22	------	
....		------	
....		------[74]	
....	23	------	
....		------[75]	
....	24a	------	
....		------[76]	
From the hands of the Champion of Jacob	24b	מיד אבר יעקב	3
From the Keeper From the Shepherd of the sons of Israel		{משמר / מרע}[77] ⌜ב⌝נ ישראל	3
From the God of thy father, who supports thee,		מאל אבכ[78] ויעזרכ	3
And El-Shaddai, who blesses thee:		ואל⌜[79]⌝ שדי ויברככ	3
Blessings of heaven above,		ברכת שמם מעל[79a]	3
Blessings of the Deep, beneath,		ברכת תהם[80] [ ]⌜מ⌝תחת	3

English	v.	Hebrew	
Blessings of breasts and womb,		ברכת שדם ורחם	3
Blessings of father and mother / man and child	26	ברכת {אב <ואם> / גבר ועל} [81]	3
Blessings of the mountains of old,		ברכת הרר[82] עד	3
Blessings of the eternal hills;		⌜ברכת⌝[83] גבעת עלם	3
Let them be on the head of Joseph		תהין[84] לראש יסף	3
On the brow of the leader of his brethren.		[85]⌜ו⌝לקדקד נזר אחו[86]	3
	Benjamin		
Benjamin is a wolf who preys,	27	בנימן זאב יטרף[87]	3
In the morning he devours spoil,		בבקר יאכל עד	3
At evening he divides booty.		[88]⌜ו⌝לערב יחלק שלל[89]	3

Notes to the Text

1. Following Prof. Albright's suggestion, we reconstruct vs. 1b-2 as a tricolon, 3:3:3. The words in vs. 1b beginning with *'ēt 'ᵃšer* and continuing to the end of the verse, seem to be a prosaic addition. In addition, *wᵉšimᶜû* after *hiqqābᵉṣû* is to be omitted, apparently having been inserted under the influence of *wᵉšimᶜû* in the second colon.

2. The pronoun is to be connected with the following phrase, in agreement with the LXX and Vulgate. On the meter, see note 4.

3. Omit the conjunction, following several LXX minuscules. According to the canons of early Canaanite and Hebrew poetry, the conjunction is used rarely at the beginning of cola.

4. The difficult phrase *yéter śᵉ'ēt* appears to be a corruption of *rē'šît*, repeated accidentally from the previous colon. The original reading of the final colon of the verse may have been either *rē'šît ᶜuzzî* (on *ᶜuzzî*, see note 5), or *yéter ᶜuzzî*. Since the present text may be more easily explained on the basis of an original *yéter*, and since that reading is supported by the versions, it is to be preferred.

Analysis indicates that the metrical structure of vs. 3 is 2:2.2:2. Note the rhyme scheme, typical of bedouin poetry, in which each colon ends with the first person pronominal suffix, *-î*.

5. Read *ᶜuzzî*, "my strength". The suffix is to be read, as indicated by the parallel expressions: *bᵉkōrî*, *kōḥî*, and *'ônî*. In עז, we have an example of early Hebrew orthography, final vowels not being indicated in the spelling. Ball, *The Book of Genesis* (*Sacred Books of the Old Testament*), Leipzig, 1896, p. 119, suggests the reading *ᶜuzzî*. In the parallel phrase, he reads *yéter śᵉ'ētî*.

6. Compare with this couplet, the Song of Lamech, Gen. 4:23-24, in which we find a similar rhyme and a similar metrical pattern.

7. Vs. 4a is unintelligible as it stands. The versions are based on an already corrupt text and offer no help in interpreting the passage. The line apparently is defective, a bicolon 3:3 being expected here (since this material goes with what follows). Possibly the first two words are to be read,

"thou art uncontrollable, like the (waters of the) sea". The next phrase is undoubtedly corrupt; cp. the similar constructions in vs. 6 with *'al*.

8. The verb *ᶜālâ* is used customarily with the preposition *ᶜal* in a construction of this type; cf. Ps. 132:3. It has been lost, apparently as the result of homoioarkton, and is to be supplied after the verb (the longer form *ᶜălê* suits the metrical requirements). The anomalous *ᶜālâ* at the end of the verse may reflect a later restoration of the missing preposition.

9. Read *miškabî*, "my bed". The word is probably singular, since the plural form, with this meaning, is always *miškābôt*. The apparent exception, *miškᵉbê* (Lev. 18:22, 20:13), is in reality a biform with a different meaning. On the displacement of *'ābîkā*, see note 11.

10. Read either the construct plural or the construct singular with the genitive case ending, following the Massoretic text. On the use of the *litterae compaginis*, see GK §90:L, and Albright, *JBL* LXI (1942), p. 117, and "The Oracles of Balaam", *JBL* LXIII (1944), p. 215, n. 48; p. 216, n. 54; etc.

11. On the shift of *'ābîkā* from the end of the first colon to the end of the second colon, see the parallel text in I Chron. 5:1, which is dependent upon this verse. Note that this rearrangement of the text clears up the obscurities in this part of the verse, and that the resulting meter is a quite regular 3:3.

12. There has been considerable discussion as to the precise significance of *'aḥḥîm* in this context. The usual interpretations emphasize either the genetic relationship (as uterine brothers) or the spiritual kinship (as partners in crime). The underlying thought probably is historical: there was a close association between the tribes historically, and in the blessing they are regarded as having a common origin and a common fate (compare the account of their joint exploits against the Shechemites in Gen. 34).

13. This word is a *hapax legomenon*. A number of different etymologies have been suggested, but as yet no satisfactory solution has been achieved. The word seems to fall into one of two possible areas of meaning: 1) it refers to some kind of weapon, possibly battle-axe, and is to be derived from the root, *kwr*, *krr*, or *krt*; 2) it is connected with the root *mkr*, and has the meaning "merchandise", and in this context, "stock in trade",

i.e., "implements of violence are their stock in trade". In this connection, note Hebrew *makkār* (II Kings 12:6,8), "broker" (so Albright), and Ugaritic *mkr* with the same meaning.

The final suffix probably is to be read -*âm*, with Sievers and Ball.

14. It is preferable to translate this colon as direct address: "Into their council enter not, O my soul! In their assembly, do not join, O my heart (lit. liver, seat of the emotions)!" Read, therefore, *tābô'î*, second feminine singular; in early orthography the final *yodh* would not be written. This reading is indicated by *tēḥad* in vs. 6a, which must be construed as a second masculine singular. For other examples of *napšî* used in direct address, see Ps. 103:1 and 104:1. Cf. Peters, "Jacob's Blessing", *JBL* VI (1886), p. 101.

15. The expression here is elliptical; *'ittâm*, "with them", is to be understood after *tēḥad*. The complete construction is to be found in Isa. 14:21. The Samaritan text, יחר, represents a revision of the Hebrew based on a misunderstanding of the syntax of the sentence; since the subject was masculine, and the sentence was read in the third person, the verb was revised to agree with the noun. Subsequently, *resh* was substituted for *daleth*, a common error at all periods of scribal transmission. The LXX reads μή ἐρίσαι τα ἤπατά μου, "let not my emotions be aroused". This interpretation is based upon the same text as the Samaritan, *yíḥar*, with the additional change to *k^ebēdî*, "my liver"; cf. note 16.

16. Read probably *k^ebēdi*, following the LXX. MT may be correct, cf. König, *Die Genesis*, Gütersloh, 1919, *ad loc.*, but the Ugaritic usage points to the other reading: *kbd*, "liver" occurs in parallel with *lb*, "heart", and *'irt*, "chest, lungs". This suggestion comes from Prof. Albright.

17. Omit *kî*, which, as it stands, impairs the symmetry of the two cola.

18. Omit the conjunction, cf. footnote 3.

19. There is no reason to look for either historical or mythological reflections in this couplet. The device used here is common to early Canaanite and Hebrew poetry. By the employment of non-exact, highly figurative language, a striking and dramatic picture is created. This is impressionistic poetry at its best. What is involved here is not a reference to the

particular slaying of men or the maiming of beasts, but a general though sharp impression of the lawlessness and violence of the two tribes. A similar idea is conveyed by the description in the Song of Lamech, Gen. 4:23-24. Other striking examples occur in Deut. 33:18 and Jud. 5:25-26. Examples from the Ugaritic literature are to be found in Gordon's *Ugaritic Handbook*, I, pp. 102ff.

Zimmern, "Der Jakobssegen und der Tierkreis", *ZA* VII (1892), pp. 161-172, finds in this verse a mythological borrowing from the Babylonian Gilgamesh. Gilgamesh and Enkidu are recorded as slaying a giant named Ḫuwawa = Ḫumbaba, the guardian of the cedar forests; and in another episode, as together killing the Bull of heaven. Following this, Ishtar pronounces a curse on Gilgamesh, and Enkidu is slain by the gods. Certainly no direct connection between the Babylonian myth and the Israelite poem exists. If there is any relationship at all, it is a remote one, and lies in the use of poetic language in the blessing which may ultimately rest upon an allusion to the heroic exploits of the Babylonian brothers-in-arms. To the composer of the blessing, the expression was a striking description of a pair of violent men. That is all it means in this context. It may possibly, however, have come down to him as a brief summary of the activities of those typical men of violence, Gilgamesh and Enkidu. See also E. Burrows, *The Oracles of Jacob and Balaam*, London, 1939; his conclusions are utterly fantastic, however. Cf. note 26.

20. The use of the first person in this blessing presents no real difficulty in interpretation. The blessing is put in the mouth of the eponymous ancestor, Jacob-Israel. On vs. 7b, see Gunkel, *Genesis*, *ad loc.*, "Jaqob selber zerstreut sie, eben durch diesen Fluch". Also see König, *Genesis*, *ad loc.*

21. In this blessing the metrical balance between parallel cola is strictly observed; it is more difficult to determine the accentual pattern. Apparently the pattern is 3:3.3:3 in vs. 5-6a; for 6b-7, a 2:2.2:2.2:2 structure emerges. The dividing line is uncertain, however, and some of these cola can be construed as having three accents. This, however, does not affect the balance between cola, where in almost every case we have an equal number of syllables.

22. Restore *hôdî*, "my majesty", or the like. A word has fallen out of the first colon, and this is the simplest emendation of the text. Written in the old orthography, *y^e^hûdâ* would have appeared as יהד; *hôdî* as הד. The loss of the second word would result from haplography.

23. Contrary to the commentaries, *'attâ* can hardly be construed in the accusative case, in apposition with the verbal suffix, -*kā*. Examples in GK §135:E of this construction are unsatisfactory, being either the result of textual corruption or not strictly applicable to the present case. According to the present Massoretic text, we must read, "Judah (art) thou; thy brothers praise thee!" On the first part of the colon, see note 22. On the structure of the blessing, see note 24.

24. The clue to the structure of this couplet is to be found in the parallelism between *yôdûkā* and *yištaḥ^a^wû*, and *'aḥḥêkā* and *b^e^nê 'ābîkā*. As the text now stands, the colon *yād^e^kā b^ec^ōrĕp 'ōy^e^bêkā* is awkwardly placed between the two cola referring to Judah's brothers; however, it fits well with the reconstructed first colon of the blessing. On the expression *b^ec^ōrĕp 'ôy^e^bêkā*, cf. Ps. 18:41 = II Sam. 22:41, and Ex. 23:27.

25. This colon has been reconstructed on the basis of the LXX, Vulgate, and Peshitta, none of which read the independent pronoun, but only the pronominal suffix, cf. note 22; on the shift of the colon from the beginning of the verse, see note 24. Apparently very early in the textual transmission of this passage, the first and third cola were confused, the present MT preserving parts of both mixed together, while the text from which the versions were made preserved only the third colon, shifted, however, to the beginning of the blessing. It is to be noted that the name "Judah" is repeated a number of times through the blessing, vs. 9 and 10, as well as in vs. 8. It seems probable that we are dealing with a collection of short blessings which once circulated independently.

25a. Cf. Isaac's blessing of Jacob in Gen. 27:29.

26. Zimmern's speculations about the different tribes and their zodiacal associations are ingenious but entirely unacceptable. It is quite certain that the zodiac did not appear in developed form until the Persian period. Even if a few of the elements which were later incorporated into the zodiacal system were known in earlier times, none of the parallels between the

signs of the zodiac and the designations of the tribes is at all convincing. Cf. Ball, *Genesis*, pp. 114ff. On the designation of Judah here, note that Dan is described as a lion's whelp in Deut. 33:22.

27. The precise meaning of this colon is not certain. The usual explanation, i.e. that the lion rises from his prey and ascends to his mountain lair, seems the best so far suggested.

28. This old poetic phrase was also applied to the nation as a whole in the Oracles of Balaam, Num. 24:9 (cf. Albright, "The Oracles of Balaam", *ad loc.*).

29. Omit the conjunction at the beginning of the second colon, *metri causa*.

30. On this construction, see Chapter IV, note 35.

31. Read *šôpēṭ*, "judge, charismatic leader", or better perhaps, following Albright, *šēpĕṭ*, Ugar. *ṯpṭ*, with the same meaning; cp. the LXX, ἄρχων. In most instances, *m^e ḥôqēq* means "commander", cf. footnote 32. In Jud. 5:14, where it clearly has this meaning, it stands in parallel, not with *šébĕṭ*, but with the "wielder of the *šébĕṭ*". In Isa. 33:22, *šôpēṭ* and *m^e ḥôqēq* are used synonymously, a fact which strongly supports the present emendation. In the early script, *pe* and *beth* were very much alike in form, and thus easily confused; by the same token they sound very much alike and the confusion may arise in oral transmission. Note that in Ps. 68:5, we have *^ca rābôt*, where the *beth* is an error, the correct original being *pe*. A striking instance of the confusion between *šébĕṭ* and *šôpēṭ* (or **šēpĕṭ*), is to be found in the parallel texts, II Sam. 7:7 = I Chron. 17:6, where II Sam. reads, incorrectly, *šibṭê*, while I Chron. preserves the correct original, *šôp^e ṭê*.

32. The meaning, "commander", is certain for *m^e ḥôqēq* in the following passages, Deut. 33:21, Jud. 5:14 (cp. Jud. 5:9, *ḥôq^e qê*, which is an abbreviation for *m^e ḥôq^e qê*, either deliberate or accidental), and Isa. 33:22. In two other instances, the meaning is not so clear, Num. 21:18 and Ps. 60:9 = Ps. 108:9. Morphologically, the word should mean, "one who issues a *ḥōq*", i.e., a commander.

33. Read with Samaritan, *d^e gālîw*, "his standards", "his battle flags". The whole phrase would read, "from the midst of his banners", an excellent parallel to *mîhûdâ* in the first colon. The expression *mibbên raglaym* is a euphemism referring to the

female genitals, cf. Deut. 28:57 (for other euphemistic usages, see lex.). The phrase in MT could only refer to the male counterparts, and indeed is so taken by the LXX and Vulgate.

34. No satisfactory solution of the problems in this bicolon has ever been presented, and there is no present prospect of a definitive solution. For a brief summary of the situation, see Skinner, *A Critical and Exegetical Commentary on Genesis* (*International Critical Commentary*), New York, 1910, pp. 519-524. G. R. Driver, "Some Hebrew Roots and their Meanings", *JTS* 23 (1922), pp. 69-73, suggests for the critical word the vocalization שֵׁיָלֹה, "prince" = Akk. *šēlu*, *šīlu*. The following reconstruction of the text may suggest the lines along which the problem should be attacked: עד[ו] (עדך) יבא שי[ ]ול יקהת עמם, *ᶜadêw* (var. *ᶜadêkā*) *yûba' šay wᵉlô yiqqᵉhat ᶜammîm*, "Unto him (unto thee) shall tribute be brought, and to him shall be the subservience of peoples".

35. Read *'ᵃsûrî*, Qal passive participle, construct, with the *hireq compaginis*; cp. Samaritan אסורי.

36. Read probably *lᵉgapnô*, "to its harness". The suffix of the third person masculine singular would not be indicated in the early orthography. The meaning "harness, trappings", for **gapn(u)* is established from the Ugaritic texts; cf. 51:IV:9-12 (= 51:IV:4-7), *mdl . ᶜr . ṣmd . pḥl . št . gpnm . dt . ksp . dt . yrq . nqbnm . ᶜdb . gpn . 'atnth .* The use of the preposition ל in the phrase *'ᵃsûrî lᵉgapnô* is not clear; if the interpretation of the passage suggested above is correct, then it must be construed as a ל of reference or agency. Cf. GK §119u, §121f; BDB, pp. 513-514.

For another interpretation of the passage which has received too little attention from scholars, see Jastrow, "Light Thrown on some Biblical Passages by Talmudic Usage", *JBL* XI (1892), pp. 126ff. Also see A. Jirku, "Der Juda-Spruch, Genesis 49:18ff, und die Texte von Ras Samra", *JPOS* 15 (1935), pp. 12-13.

37. Read *ᶜêrô* < *ᶜayrô*, Ugar. *ᶜr*. The preservation of the *he* to indicate the third masculine singular suffix reflects 9th-6th century B.C. spelling practice.

38. Omit the conjunction at the beginning of the second colon.

39. There is no evidence for a feminine form of this word, the other occurrences of this word in the Bible being masculine. The final *he* is to be regarded therefore as the third masculine singular suffix (agreeing with the masculine *b^{e}nî '^{a}tōnō*); on the orthography, see footnote 37.

40. Note the preservation of the archaic case ending in the *nomen regens* of a construct chain, a not uncommon feature of early Hebrew poetry. On the bicolon as a whole, compare Zech. 9:9.

41. Omit the *waw*, possibly a case of dittography.

42. The word means clearly, "mantle, garment", and is found in the Kilamuwa inscription from the late ninth century, line 8, סות (the waw is consonantal), and in the Batno^{c}am inscription. Cf. P. Joüon, "Gen. 49:11 סוּת", *Biblica* 21 (1940), p. 58, among others on סות and its vocalization. Samaritan כסותה seems to be an ancient emendation. On the final *he*, see note 37.

43. This is apparently a construct chain, cf. footnote 40, to be rendered literally, "darkness of eyes more than wine"; cp. the LXX paraphrase, "his eyes are darker than wine". For the meaning of *ḥaklîlî*, note Akk. *eklu*, *eklītu*, "dark, darkness". Cp. Prov. 23:29, where חכלילות means "darkness", but with the specific sense of "bloodshot". The Samaritan חכלילו is either a misspelling (*waw* and *yodh* are almost identical in the Herodian script), or it may preserve the original and correct nominative case ending, *-u*.

44. Omit the *waw* at the beginning of the second colon.

45. This expression shows that the preposition is used with the adjective in a comparative sense, i.e., "teeth whiter than milk", rather than "teeth made white by milk". So Jastrow and others.

The description in vs. 11 may well have a Canaanite mythical background; cf. Sellin, "Zu dem Judasspruch im Jaqobssegen Gen. 49:8-12 und im Mosesegen Deut. 33:7" *ZAW* 60 (1944), pp. 57-67, esp. p. 63. Sellin's attempts to date the Judah blessings in Gen. 49 and Deut. 33 are, however, most unfortunate.

46. Both in MT and in the reconstructed text presented here, the word *z^{e}bûlûn* stands as extra-metrical. This is not to be regarded as a hypothetical occurrence in Hebrew poetry, since such extra-metrical feet are a common device in the Ugaritic

epics; cf. Ginsberg, *Orientalia* 5 (1936), pp. 171ff. In Deut. 33, in two instances, the name of the tribe is not included in the blessing itself (Benjamin, vs. 12, and Joseph, vs. 13). Presumably the name stood at the beginning of the blessing (disregarding the titles which now stand in MT, a later development in the transmission of the blessings), as an extra-metrical heading. In time this practice was generalized, and headings were attached to the other blessings, whether the tribe was named in the body of the blessing or not.

47. This bicolon is reconstructed on the basis of Jud. 5:17, where the complete text is preserved. By a slight rearrangement of the words (i.e., *yāšab* after *yammîm*) the omission in Gen. 49 becomes explicable as a case of homoioarkton. The description was applicable to the whole area in which the tribes of Asher and Zebulun were located, and could therefore be used with equal facility for either.

48. The word *ḥōp* does not belong in this context. In every other instance in the Bible, it is coupled with the word for "sea" (as in vs. 13a); its insertion here is the result of dittography. It has been suggested by a number of scholars that לחף is a corruption of חבל, and that is quite possible. Equally possible, and perhaps preferable, is the reading לפף, suggested by Prof. Albright. The colon would then read "And he indeed doth fare on ships". Cf. לפף שבל, at the end of the Ahiram inscription, which is to be translated "wayfarer"; Albright, "The Phoenician Inscriptions of the Tenth Century B.C. from Byblus", p. 155.

49. As it stands, this bicolon makes no satisfactory sense. There is no parallelism between the cola, and the geographical reference is wrong on topographical grounds (i.e., Zebulun did not extend to Sidon, so על or עד are incorrect). If the first colon is restored in accordance with the suggestion above (note 48): *w^{e}hû' lôpēp '^{a}niyyôt*, then some equivalent idea must be present in the second colon. On the basis of Isa. 33:21 (cp. Num. 24:24), <צי> is restored before צידן, its loss being due to simple haplography. In this context, ירכת is impossible; the least drastic emendation would be ירכב. The resulting text is, *yirkab ^{c}al ṣiyyê Ṣîdôn*. The use of *rkb* for travelling on ships is frequent in Akkadian, and regular in Arabic. The full bicolon would then be translated:

And he is a sailor of ships
He rides on the vessels of Sidon.

50. This word remains obscure. The usual interpretation, "bony", i.e., "strong", is unsatisfactory. The best recent treatment of the phrase *ḥămōr gārĕm* is that of Feigin, "Hamor Garim, 'Castrated Ass'", *JNES* V (1946), pp. 230-233. It is possible, however, to emend the text slightly, and read *ḥ^a^mōr gīdîm*, "sinewy ass"; this makes better sense in the context.

51. Omit the article, which is a later insertion. It is not found in early Hebrew or Canaanite poetry.

52. This word occurs in three early passages of Hebrew poetry: Jud. 5:16, Ps. 68:14 (without the *mem* preformative), and here. It is presumably to be associated with *'ašpōt*, "rubbish heap". On the etymology of the term, cf. Albright, "The Earliest Forms of Hebrew Verse", *JPOS* II (1922), p. 78, n. 2.

53. Omit the conjunction at the beginning of the cola, as in the Vulgate. Read *yir'ê*, "he saw". In the early orthography, the final *he* would not have been written.

54. Read *m^e^nûḥô*, "his resting-place", following a number of scholars. The third masculine singular suffix was indicated by *he* in pre-exilic times, cf. footnote 37. This is implied by the masculine adjective *ṭôb*. The Peshitta also reads the suffix here; cf. footnote 56. The Samaritan offers a variant text, מנוחה and טובה; the LXX and Vulgate have the same interpretation of the text.

55. The *nota accusativi* and article reflect a later revision of the text; these may have been introduced to balance the meter in a defective line, since something has apparently dropped out. It is suggested that *yabbîṭ*, "he looked upon", has fallen out by haplography. Note that the three preceding letters (in pre-exilic orthography) are *yodh*, *teth*, and *beth*. It is unnecessary to point out that *rā'â* and *hibbîṭ* are used consistently in parallel construction throughout the Bible.

56. Read *'arṣô*, "his land", following the Syriac, cf. footnote 54. The final vowel would not be indicated in tenth century orthography.

57. Omit the conjunction (cf. LXX). Read *yiṭṭê*; the *he* would not have appeared in early orthography.

58. On the expression, *mas ^c^ôbēd*, see the thorough treatment by I. Mendelsohn, "State Slavery in Ancient Palestine",

BASOR #85 (1942), pp. 14-17, and *Slavery in the Ancient Near East*, New York, 1949. It refers to a variety of state slavery in which the corvée workers were reduced to the status of slaves. This was not practiced in Israel until the time of David and Solomon, and then only upon subjugated non-Israelites. The instance here must refer to the subjection of Issachar to the Canaanites at an early period of the occupation, or perhaps to the Philistines toward the end of the period of the Judges. Conceivably this may reflect the situation of certain Hebrew groups in Palestine before the conquest.

59. This colon is considerably shorter than the following one; on the analogy of vs. 19, and based upon a common construction with the verb *dîn*, we supply the noun *dîn* after *yādîn* (lost by haplography). The passage then reads, "Dan will plead the cause of his people". Compare the following passages: Jer. 5:28, 22:16, 30:13; in Ugaritic, 127:33-34 = 127:45-47,

la-tadīnu dīn(a) 'almanati
la-taṯpuṭu ṯipṭa qaṣir(i) napši.

60. Vs. 17 constitutes a separate blessing, not directly connected with the previous one. Omit *y^e^hî*, which is superfluous, disturbing the meter and the meaning.

61. The LXX apparently read *^c^āqēb* (singular), here; cp. also the Peshitta, which paraphrases. This may reflect the older spelling practice, in which the final vowel letters were not written; or it may be a correction on the basis of a literal interpretation of the passage (i.e., the snake bites only one heel), whereas the real meaning is less prosaic: "Who snaps at the heels of the horse ..." The phrase *^c^iqbê sûs* occurs also in the Song of Deborah, Jud. 5:22.

62. Read *way-yappēl*, following Ball (on the basis of the Peshitta, ܘܢܦܠ).

63. The LXX apparently read *rôkēb*; this may reflect the older orthography, in which the final vowel would not be indicated. The clear implication of the passage is that the horse, attacked by the snake, bolts and throws its rider. This scene may reflect any period in the history of Palestine after the Hyksos (18th century B.C.), who introduced horses and chariots in considerable numbers. It is true that cavalry was not used in Palestine until the ninth century, but there was a long period of informal or non-military horseback riding before that. A good illustration of horseback riding in the Amarna Age is to

be found in Letter No. 245, in which Biridiya of Megiddo tells how his mare was shot by an arrow and felled. Cf. Knudtzon, *El-Amarna Tafeln*, I, Leipzig, 1915, pp. 292-93, Biridiya of Megiddo to the King #4 (Prof. Albright).

64. The metrical structure of the couplet (vs. 17) presents a problem. It consists of a pair of bicola, which may be construed as either 2:2.2:2 or 3:3.3:3. In the former case, the first three cola present no particular difficulty, but the last one clearly has three stresses; in the latter case, the first, third, and fourth cola are satisfactory, but the second has only two stresses. Nevertheless, the requirements of symmetry are amply met, and an almost perfect balance obtains in the couplet as it stands. Note that there is practically no variation in the number of syllables in each of the four cola.

65. This verse does not belong with the Blessing of Dan, nor is it an original part of the blessings as a group. It seems to be a liturgical rubric inserted approximately at the midpoint in the series of blessings, when the poem was adapted for use in worship.

66. The word *g^{e}dûd* is to be construed as a predicate nominative with *gād*. Contrary to the commentators, the play on words must turn on the characterization of Gad, not his enemies. This is confirmed by the other blessings in the poem, in which the tribes are characterized under different figures: Judah, vs. 9, Issachar, vs. 14, Dan, vs. 17, Naphtali, vs. 21, and Benjamin, vs. 27.

67. Read *y^{e}gûdan(na)*, the energic form without the suffix. This is a common construction in Ugaritic, and occurs a number of times in early Israelite poetry as well, cf. Chapter IV, note 25 for examples from the Blessing of Moses and references to the Oracles of Balaam (Num. 23:9,19,20; 24:17, see Albright, "The Oracles of Balaam", *passim*). The dropping of the suffix removes the grammatical difficulties inherent in the usual rendering of the colon; cf. footnote 87.

68. The *mem* at the beginning of vs. 20 does not belong there (so the LXX, Vulgate, Peshitta, and all scholars), but rather at the end of vs. 19, with *^{c}āqēb*. It is probably to be construed as an adverbial formation (as commonly in Ugaritic and Hebrew), "from the rear, at the rear"; cp. Vulgate,

"retrorsum". On the other hand, the *mem* may be enclitic; note that the Peshitta omits it entirely, ܚܡܪܐ.

69. See footnote 68.

70. MT presents a conflate text, as indicated by the disagreement in gender. One variant is preserved in the Samaritan text, שמן לחמו (so also the LXX and Vulgate). The other is preserved in the Peshitta and Targum; the Hebrew text underlying these apparently read שמנה ארצו; cf. Ugar. ᶜAnat II:39, Gen. 27:28, etc. The word *léḥem* is used in its basic sense, of "food".

71. Omit *wᵉhû*, which has been inserted in the text as a result of dittography (note the rendering of the Vulgate). This is suggested by metrical considerations.

72. It is also possible to read the Qal passive, *yuttan*, "he receives".

73. The present text is unsatisfactory in many respects. Of the suggested emendations, the best involves the change of *'ayyālâ* to *'ēlâ*, and *'imrê* to *'ᵃmīrê* (cf. Skinner, *Genesis*, *ad loc.*). In addition, the following readings commend themselves: *šillᵉḥâ* for *šᵉlûḥâ*, and *nātᵉnâ* for *han-nôtēn*, dropping the initial *he* as a case of dittography; the final *â* would not be indicated in the older orthography. The resulting text is

Naphtali is a terebinth which produces,	נפתל אל שלח
Which puts forth beautiful foliage;	נתנ אמר שפר

This reconstructed text is based generally upon the LXX: Νεφθαλι στέλεχος ἀνειμένον ἐπιδιδοὺς ἐν τῷ γενήματι κάλος. This, however, does not necessarily reflect the Hebrew text given above. For *'ēlâ*, we would normally expect δρῦς or τερέβινθος, not στέλεχος, which stands for Hebrew *ᶜālê*, *géza*ᶜ, etc. In conclusion, while the proposed text is plausible, it is not entirely convincing. In the present state of our knowledge, perhaps nothing better can be attained. Cf. Barnes, "A Taunt-Song in Gen. XLIX:20,21", *JTS* 33 (1932), pp. 354-59.

74. This verse is hopelessly corrupt, as witness the versions and commentaries. Some suggestions may be in order, however. The verse consists of a tricolon, the first two cola of which present the familiar poetic pattern, abc:abd. The most recent and complete treatment of this pattern in Ugaritic and Hebrew poetry is to be found in Albright's "The Psalm of Habakkuk", soon to appear in the T. H. Robinson Anniversary Volume.

MT *ben* is to be read with the case ending, *metri causa*, as in the Oracles of Balaam, Num. 24:3, 15, cf. Albright, "The Oracles of Balaam", p. 216, n. 54. The word *pōrāt* is unintelligible as it stands, none of the suggested interpretations having any real merit. That the text may nevertheless be correct is indicated by the occurrence of the name *prt* in Ugaritic (cf. Gordon, *Ugaritic Handbook*, Text No. 315:4), and also the combination *bn . prtn*, Text 400:III:9.

The phrase ^{ca}*lê* ^{c}*ayin* is to be connected with ^{ca}*lê šûr*, on which see the discussion below.

In the third colon, MT בנות צעדה and Samaritan בני צעירי are both in need of correction. Samaritan בני, "my son", is perhaps correct. The *taw* in MT is to be taken with the following verb, to be read either as a Qal imperfect, *tiṣ*^{c}*ad*, "thou dost march", or the emphatic imperative, *ṣa*^{c}*dâ*, "march". In early poetry, this verb is used in a martial sense, cf. Jud. 5:4 = Ps. 68:8. With the preposition ^{ca}*lê*, this suggests a military attack. The chief targets in an attack upon a city would be the water supply (^{c}*ayin*), and the wall (*šûr*). In spite of considerable obscurities in vs. 23-24, the same picture of military struggle is given.

75. This verse presents no serious difficulties in itself; the chief problem is to relate it to the surrounding material; cf. notes 74 and 76. The single emendation of MT is taken from the Samaritan, ירריבהו, *y*^{e}*rîbûhû*, "they strive against him", for *wārobbû*. This improves the meter as well as the meaning. The *ba*^{ca}*lê ḥiṣṣîm* presumably are archers, though the expression is unique in the Bible.

76. Verse 24a has defied the best efforts of scholars for many years. Nothing satisfactory has resulted. The versions only add to the confusion.

77. As recognized by most scholars, MT does not make sense, and is also overly long. In the first two words of the colon, משם רעה, there is a conflate reading. One or two letters have dropped out by haplography, the original variants being *miššômēr* and *mêrô*^{c}*ê*; written out in early orthography the text would have appeared something like this, משמ<ר>רע or משמר<מ>רע. The word אבן is impossible in this context. What is required is a parallel to *ya*^{c}*qōb*, and "Israel-stone", whatever that might mean, will not do. The simplest emendation is to read *b*^{e}*nê* (בנ)

for *'ébĕn*; the intrusion of the *aleph* might be due to the influence of אבר in the first colon of 24b. On Yahweh as the *šômēr yiśrā'ēl*, cf. Ps. 121:4, and as the *rô^cê yiśrā'ēl*, Ps. 80:2. Cp. Gunkel's treatment, *Genesis*, p. 427. A somewhat different reconstruction of the text, though along similar lines, is offered by Morgenstern in his "Divine Triad in Biblical Mythology", *JBL* LXIV (1945), p. 25.

78. Grammatically, the expression may be understood as either, "from the God of thy father", or "from El, thy father". In the present context, the former is perhaps preferable; in support of this reading, see the parallel expression in Ex. 15:2, אלהי אבי. On the second rendering, cf. Morgenstern, "Divine Triad in Biblical Mythology", p. 25. There are a number of references in the OT to God as the father of his people, or of different individuals, viz. Deut. 32:6, etc.

79. Read *w^e'ēl*, with three Hebrew mss., Samaritan and the Peshitta (ܘܐܠܗܝ); the LXX has ὁ θεὸς ὁ ἐμὸς, the Vulgate, *et Omnipotens*. See, however, Morgenstern's remarks, "Divine Triad in Biblical Mythology", pp. 25-26.

79a. Cf. Gen. 27:39b; Deut. 33:13, Chapter IV, note 43.

80. The bicolon (vs. 25b) is parallel to Deut. 33:13 on which see Chapter IV, *ad loc*. In its present form, the second colon here is too long, having been harmonized with the parallel in Deut. 33. In Deut. 33:13, the word *mégĕd* = *birkôt* has been omitted; in Gen. 49, presumably one of the other words ought to be dropped, *rôbéṣĕt* (thus preserving the parallelism with the first colon, and removing the metrical difficulty). In dealing with cases of parallel transmission, the earliest written form of the texts would exhibit the widest divergence; over the years, in the process of transmission, the tendency would be toward harmonizing the differences. The common original would lie much further back when the poem circulated in oral form.

The LXX offers a variant to this colon, καὶ εὐλογίαν γῆς ἐχούσης πάντα, which is equivalent to Deut. 33:16a. It may be a genuine variant, indicating the parallel between heaven and earth, and not simply an inner corruption in the transmission of the Greek mss., due to the influence of the passage in Deuteronomy. Note that the LXX of Gen. 49:25b does not correspond at all with that of Deut. 33:16a in so far as the wording is concerned.

This shifting of the particular blessings would point to the relatively fluid character of the original blessing. It probably appeared in a number of forms, of which only the two in Gen. 49 and Deut. 33 have survived. Besides the material common to both, certain blessings are peculiar to each recension. This suggests that the common original was somewhat longer than either, and probably differed from both. See our remarks in Chapter IV, note 41. For this reason, it is difficult to accept, in principle, I. Sonne's attempt to harmonize the texts of Deut. 33:13-15 and Gen. 49:25-26, in his "Genesis 49:25-26", *JBL* LXV (1946), pp. 303-306. In particular details the two texts may be useful in correcting each other; but there is as much reason to expect differences in the order and content of the blessings as similarities.

81. Vs. 26a, ברכת אביך גברו על, must stand in parallel with vs. 25c, ברכת שדים ורחם. The difficulties in the text are serious, however. The best line of approach is offered by Gunkel, who reads בִּרְכֹת אָב אַךְ גֶּבֶר וָעוּל, *Genesis*, *ad loc*. Morgenstern's rendering improves the meter by the omission of *'ābîkā*, "Divine Triad in Biblical Mythology", pp. 25-26. Sonne's reading is unacceptable. On the basis of the Samaritan and Morgenstern's correction of Gunkel's rendering, it is possible to see in MT a defective conflate text. One variant read, in accordance with the Samaritan and the LXX, ברכת אב ואם (the omission of אם in MT is due to homoioarkton; the suffix is not expected, because of the general terms in the parallel colon, and probably came in under the influence of *'ābîkā* in vs. 25a; metrical considerations are also involved). The other variant corresponds roughly to Morgenstern's text, ברכת גבר ועֻל. The second variant seems to provide a better parallel to the first colon. The first variant may originally have formed part of another blessing.

82. With most scholars, and following Hab. 3:6, we read here, *harᵃrê ᶜad*. Compare the parallel phrases in Deut. 33:15, Num. 23:7, Chapter IV, notes 51 and 52.

83. For *ta'ᵃwat*, read *birkôt*, as indicated by the constant repetition of *birkôt* through the blessing. תאות is presumably a corruption of *tᵉbû'ôt* (cf. Deut. 33:14), which has been brought into the text. See Skinner's discussion, *Genesis*, p. 532. It should be pointed out that the LXX reads εὐλογίαις = *birkôt*.

84. Read **tihyan(na)*, Qal third feminine singular jussive, with a collective subject (*birkôt*); cp. the parallel Deut. 33:16, Chapter IV, n. 55. On the use of energic *nun* without the pronominal suffix, see footnote 67.

85. Omit the conjunction at the beginning of the second colon.

86. On the blessing as a whole, cf. Chapter IV, note 41.

87. Note that in the first colon, there is a relative clause without the relative particle. This is a common construction in early Hebrew poetry, and is the basis for our reconstruction of the first colon of the blessing on Gad, cf. footnote 67.

88. Omit the conjunction at the beginning of cola.

89. The blessing on Benjamin is a tricolon, 3:3:3. Cp. the blessing of Benjamin in Deut. 33:12, and Naphtali, Deut. 33:23.

CHAPTER IV

THE BLESSING OF MOSES

CHAPTER IV

THE BLESSING OF MOSES[a]

Detailed discussion of the literature on the Blessing of Moses will be found in the notes to the text. The best of the older treatments is that of Cassuto (1928).[b] T. H. Gaster has written most recently on Deut. 33, but restricts himself to the framework of the poem (vss. 3-5, 26-29).[c]

An analysis of the text has shown that the Blessing originally was written in the orthography of the tenth century. The writers have attempted a reconstruction of the text, restoring as accurately as possible the purely consonantal spelling used in Israel at that time. Explanations will be found in the notes. In addition to orthographic archaisms, a number of other archaic features are to be found in the Blessing. These, particularly poetic diction and structure, find their closest parallels in what is acknowledged to be the oldest Israelite poetry. Further, the ode which frames the blessings, and some of the blessings themselves (like those in the Blessing of Jacob), have strong affinities with the Canaanite literature which influenced Israel's early poetic genius.

On the basis of these considerations, we hold that this Blessing, like the Blessing of Jacob, was composed, most probably, in the eleventh century B.C.[d] It may not have been written down, however, until the tenth century,[e] during the period of literary and scribal activity which accompanied the reigns of David and Solomon.[f]

Notes to the Introduction

a. This chapter is a slightly revised version of an article entitled "The Blessing of Moses", by Frank M. Cross Jr. and David Noel Freedman, which appeared in the *Journal of Biblical Literature*, LXVII (1948), pp. 191-210.

b. U. Cassuto, "Il cap. 33 del Deuteronomio e la festa del Capo d'anno nel' antico Israele," *Revista degli Studi Orientali*, XI (1928), pp. 233-253. Nevertheless, all treatments before 1944 have been antiquated by the new developments.

c. T. H. Gaster, "An Ancient Eulogy on Israel: Deuteronomy 33:3-5, 26-29", *JBL*, LXVI (1947), pp. 53-62. R. Gordis has since published a criticism of this treatment, "The Text and Meaning of Deuteronomy 33:27", *JBL*, LXVII (1948), pp. 69-72. Gordis, for the most part, repeats material originally issued in 1933, "Critical Notes on the Blessing of Moses (Deut xxxiii)", *JTS*, XXXIV, pp. 390-392.

A brief note by H. L. Ginsberg in *BASOR* #110 (1948) may also be mentioned.

d. Cf. W. J. Phythian-Adams, "On the Date of the 'Blessing of Moses'", *JPOS*, III (1923), pp. 158-166. He defends a similar date on wholly different grounds.

e. The orthographic evidence tends to fix the tenth century as the *terminus ad quem*. The change from purely consonantal spelling to the general use of *matres lectionis* to indicate *final* vowels was complete in the ninth century. This should not be confused with the gradual introduction of internal vowel letters at a much later date.

f. For comparisons with the Blessing of Jacob, and discussion of the literary category to which this poem belongs, see the introduction to the Blessing of Jacob, Chapter III.

The Blessing of Moses[1]

Yahweh from Sinai came	2	יהו[2] מסנ[3] בא	3
He beamed forth from Seir		[4]ו⌈זרח משער ...[5]	3
.....			
He shone from Mount Paran.		הפע מהר פרן[6]	3
With him were myriads of holy ones		[7]ו⌈את-מ[8] רבבת קדש<ם>[9]	3
At his right hand proceeded the mighty ones		מימנ[10] אשד אלם[11]	3
Yea, the guardians of the peoples.	3	[12]אף חבב[13] עמם	3
All the holy ones are at thy hand		כל קדש<ם>[14] בידכ[15]	3
They prostrate themselves at thy feet		ו⌈המתכ[16] לרגלכ	3
They carry out thy decisions.		ישא-מ[17] דברתכ[18] [19]	3

....	-------------
[20]	-------------

Reuben

Let Reuben live, let him not die	6	יח ראבן[21] ו⌈אל ימת	3
Although his men be few.		ויהי[22] מתו מספר[23]	3

Judah

Hearken, Yahweh, to the voice of Judah	7	שמע יהו קל-יהד[24]	3
And to his people come thou!		ואל עמ תבאן[25]	3
....		[26]------------	3
And a help from his foes be thou!		ועזר מצרו תהי[27]	3

Levi

....		28-------------	
Bless, Yahweh, his might	11	[29]ברך יהו חל	3
The works of his hands accept thou!		[30]⌈פעל [31]ידו תרצ	3
Smite the loins of his foes		מחץ[32] מתנ-מ[33] קמו	3
His enemies, whoever attacks him.		[34]⌈משנאו מן יקמנ[35]	3

Benjamin

The beloved of Yahweh encamps in safety	12	ידד-יהו [36]ישכן[37] לבטח	3
The Exalted One hovers over him		[38]על⌉ חפפ עלו [39][]	3
And between his shoulders he tents.		ובן כתפו שכן[40]	3

Joseph[41]

Blessed of Yahweh is his land	13	מברכת יהו ארצ	3
From the abundance of the heavens above		[42]ממגד שמם מעל⌉[43]	3
From the Deep crouching beneath		⌈מתהם[44] רבצת[45] תחת	3
From the abundance of the harvests of the sun	14	[46]⌈ממגד תבאת שמש[47]	3
From the abundance of the yields of the moon		⌈ממגד גרש[48] ירח⌉[49]	3
From the abundance of the ancient mountains	15	ממגד[50] הרר[51] קדם	3
From the abundance of the eternal hills		⌈ממגד גבעת עלם[52]	3

From the abundance of the earth and its fullness	16	ממגד ארץ ומלאה	3
And the favor of the One who tented on Sinai		ורצן שכנ[53] סנ[54]	3
May it be on the head of Joseph		תבא[55] / תה לראש יספ	3
On the brow of the leader of his brethren.		לקדקד[56] נזר אחו	3
His first-born bull, majesty is his	17	בכר שר[57] הדר-ל	3
The horns of the wild bull are his horns		[58]קרנ ראמ[59] קרנו	3
With them, the nations he gores		בהם עמם ינגח	3
He attacks the ends of the earth		ידח[60] אפס[61] ארץ	3
Behold the myriads of Ephraim!		[62]הם רבבת אפרם	3
Behold the thousands of Manasseh!		הם אלפ מנש[63]	3

Zebulun

Exult, Zebulun, in thy going forth	18	שמח זבלן בצאתכ	3
Rejoice, Issachar, in thy tents.		[64]שש ישׂשכר באהלכ	3
....		[65]______________	

Gad

Blessed be the broad lands of Gad	20	ברך מרחב[66] גד	3
Gad as a lioness lies in wait		גד[67] כלבא[68] שכן	3
He tears the arm, the head as well		[69]טרפ זרע אפ-קדקד	3

And he seeks out the finest for himself	21	[70]וירא ראשת ל	3
For he pants after a commander's share.		כ ישם[71] חלקת מחקק[72]	3
....		[73]____________	

Dan

Dan is a lion's whelp	22	דן גר ארי	2
Who shies away from a viper.		יזנק [74]מי⌜בשן	2

Naphtali

Naphtali is satisfied with favor	23	נפתל שבע רצן	3
And full of the blessing of Yahweh		ומלא ברכת יהו	3
West and South he will inherit.		ימ[75] ודרם ירש[76]	3

Asher

Most blessed of the sons is Asher	24	ברך מבנם אשר	3
He is the favorite of his brothers		יהי[77] רצי אחו	3
He dips his feet in oil.		[78]י⌜טבל בשמן רגלו[79]	3
....		[80]_____________	

There is none like the God of Jeshurun	26	אן <אל>[81] כאל ישרן	3
Who rides the heavens mightily		[82]רכב שמם בעז	3
Who rides gloriously the clouds.		רכ<ב> ⌜בגאת שחקם	3

His (Jeshurun's) refuge is the God of old	27	מענ[83] אלה קדם	3
Under him are the arms of the Eternal.		⸢⸣מתחת<ר>[84] זרעת עלמ[85]	3
And he drove out before thee the enemy.		ויגרש מפנכ איב	3
....		[86]------------	
Israel encamps in safety	28	⸢⸣ישכן ישראל בטח	3
Securely apart dwells Jacob		בדד ען[87] יעקב	3
Upon his land are grain and wine		[88]<על> ארץ דגן ותרש[89]	3
Yea, his heavens drip down dew.		אף-שמו יערפ טל	3
	29		
Happy art thou, O Israel / O Israel, who is like thee		[90]אשרכ ישראל / ישראל מ-כמכ	2
A people who found safety in Yahweh		עם נשע ביהו	2
Whose shield is thy help		מגנ[91] עזרכ	2
Whose sword is thy glory.		[]חרב גאתכ	2
Thine enemies fawn upon thee		[92]⸢יכחש איבכ לכ	3
But thou upon their backs dost tread.		ואת על-במתמ[93] תדרך	3

Notes to the Text

1. In the reconstruction of the text, marks of accentuation have been omitted. The problems of early Hebrew vocalization and accentuation have not entirely been solved. While the Massoretic pointing provides an adequate basis for the indication of stress-syllables, it is not correct in a large number of cases. It is clear, furthermore, that in poetry there was considerably more freedom with regard to the placing of the tone than in prose, and that accentuation was influenced seriously by metrical considerations.

The number of stresses in each colon is indicated in the right-hand margin. The prevailing metrical form in the Blessing of Moses is a bicolon, 3:3, as in vs. 14-17, etc. A considerable number of tricola, 3:3:3, occur as well, e.g., vss. 2-3, 12, 26. On the prevalence of this form in Ugaritic and early Hebrew poetry, see Albright, "The Old Testament and the Canaanite Language and Literature", pp. 23ff., and the forthcoming article on "The Psalm of Habakkuk". There are also a few cases of bicola, 2:2, e.g., vss. 22, 29.

Symmetry (*parallelismus membrorum*) is the dominant feature of Hebrew poetry. This is true not only with regard to the meaning of parallel cola, but also their structure and length. While early Israelite poets, in all probability, did not count syllables, their verses nevertheless were carefully balanced. Parallel cola frequently have the same number of syllables (cf. the discussion in Chapter I). In the Blessing of Moses, there is an *average* maximum divergence of *one* syllable. Other general conclusions are as follows: 1) There may be *one* or *two* syllables between stresses, but not *three*; 2) As a result, a two-stress colon will contain from *four* to *six* syllables, a three-stress colon, from *six* to *nine* syllables.

It must be emphasized that these rules cannot be applied rigidly. In the first place, we may expect to find a number of exceptions, deliberately introduced into the text to produce special effects; e.g., vs. 22, where three of the four cola have three syllables, while the first consists of the monosyllable *dān*, and receives added emphasis. In the second place, we know very little about the word-forms peculiar to Hebrew poetry. Irregularities in meter may be due to the fact that normal prose forms have been substituted in the Massoretic text for longer or shorter forms in the original poem. This is especially true of words with case endings. Several of these are still preserved (*metri causa*) in the Massoretic and Samaritan texts of Deut. 33. How many others were in the original poem, but lost in the process of textual revision and transmission, cannot accurately be determined. Lastly, we must allow for deep-seated corruptions in the present text.

It is becoming increasingly clear that the early poetry of Israel, like that of Ugarit, was quite regular in structure, and susceptible to quantitative analysis.

2. The tetragrammaton is found as early as cir. 840 B.C., on the Mesha Stone. In the consonantal spelling of the tenth century, however, the *mater lectionis he* for the final vowel is not expected. Earlier, the spelling would have been with final *yodh* (**yhwy*).

3. In all probability, vocalize *mis-sînê*. Diphthongs regularly were contracted in Old Canaanite, Phoenician, and North Israelite, (*ay* > *ê*; *aw* > *ô*). The etymology of the word, however, remains obscure, cf. note 54. A parallel case is שַׁדַּי pronounced **šaddê* (*sadde* in Egyptian transliteration); cf. the discussion in the introduction to Chapter V.

4. Omit the conjunction.

5. *lāmô* is difficult, and the text may be corrupt. A word is required, however, for metrical reasons. The versions read, "to us". Bertholet, *Deuteronomium* (*Kurzer Hand-Commentar zum Alten Testament*; Leipzig and Tübingen, 1899), p. 104; Budde, *Der Segen Mose's*, Tübingen, 1922, p. 17; Gressmann, *Die Schriften des Alten Testaments*, Göttingen, 1922, II, p. 173, and others emend the text to read לְעַמּוֹ. Cassuto, however, follows the versions, and reads לָנוּ, "Il cap. 33 del Deuteronomio", pp. 235f. Nyberg's elaborate attempt to explain the Massoretic text is not convincing ("Deuteronomium 33:2-3", *ZDMG*, 92 [1938], pp. 320ff.). At present, no solution recommends itself.

6. Yahweh's association with mountains is a frequent theme of the poetry of this period. These theophanies are couched generally in the imagery of natural cataclysm. Cf. Jud. 5:4-5; Ps. 68:7-9, 15-17; Hab. 3:3-15; Ps. 18:8-16.

7. Omit the *waw*, "and"; see footnote 4.

8. Vocalize *'ittô-m ribᵉbôt qᵉdōšîm*. This rendering follows the Targums, the Vulgate, and in part the LXX (σὺν

μυριάσιν κάδης). Three stages in the orthography of the first word, *'ittô*, may be noted. In the tenth century, it would have been written simply את; this may be the basis for the Greek translation σύν. The Massoretic text preserves the spelling of later pre-exilic times, אתה; *he* is regularly used to represent the third-person masculine singular suffix, -*ô*, in the Siloam Inscription and the Lachish Ostraca. There are numerous instances in the biblical text as well, cf. S. R. Driver, *Notes on the Hebrew Text of the Books of Samuel* (2nd ed.; Oxford, 1913), pp. xxxii-xxxiii. The Samaritan text, finally, reflects the post-exilic revision of the orthography, with final -*ô* being indicated by *waw* instead of *he*. On the *mem* as enclitic (= enclitic *mi* of the Amarna Letters and the Ugaritic Texts), see H. L. Ginsberg, *The Ugarit Texts* [Hebrew], Jerusalem, 1936, p. 130; W. F. Albright, "The Oracles of Balaam", p. 215, n. 45, and "The Old Testament and the Canaanite Language and Literature", pp. 23f.; T. H. Gaster, "Psalm 29", *JQR*, NS XXXVII (1946), p. 65, n. 32.

9. Vocalize *q*^{e}*dōšîm*, the final *mem* having been lost by haplography. The emended reading is supported by Targum Onkelos (קדישין). This term is commonly used for the members of the divine assembly in both biblical and extra-biblical literature.

10. *mîmînô* frequently has the meaning "at his right (side)"; cf. S. R. Driver, *Deuteronomy* (*ICC*), p. 390, although his interpretation is different. Compare the passage in I Kings 22:19, "... I saw Yahweh sitting upon his throne, and all the host of heaven standing about him, on his right and on his left (*mîmînô u-miśś*^{e}*môlô*)".

11. The Massoretic text, אשדת למו, is very obscure. Conjectures are almost as numerous as scholars. The suggested reading is אשר אלם (omitting the final *waw*, which as a vowel letter, would not have appeared in tenth-century orthography), *'āš*^{e}*rû 'ēlîm*, "... proceeded the mighty ones". If this was the original reading, the present corruption of the text may be explained on the basis of the following diagram, restoring the script of the tenth-ninth centuries.

It will be noticed that slight damage (i.e., a smear) to the original text (-רא-), could easily produce the present -דת-.

With regard to the verb אשר, compare Prov. 9:6; an interesting parallel comes from KRT A:92-93, *hlk . l'alpm . ḥṯṯ . wlrbt . kmyr . 'aṯr*, "They march in thousands ..., and in myriads ... they proceed". *'ēlîm* and *qedōšîm* occur in parallel cola in contemporary literature, cf. Ps. 89:6-8, Ex. 15:11 (LXX and Peshitta). For passages with the same poetic motif, see Jud. 5:4 and Hab. 3:5. The latter is rendered by Prof. Albright, "Before Him Pestilence marched, and Plague went forth at His feet".

12. This colon is noticeably shorter than those which precede and follow. Read possibly *'appû* or *'āpepû*, "surround, encompass, gather round". The meaning of the stem is clear from its usage in parallel with *sbb*, Ps. 18:5,6 = II Sam. 22:5,6; Jonah 2:6; cp. also Acc. *apâpu* and *uppu*. The passage would then read, "Gathered round (him) the guardians of the peoples".

13. Vocalize *ḥôbebî* (i.e., masculine construct plural, cf. Chapter V, note 4) *ʿammîm*, "the ones who care for the peoples", the guardians of the peoples; cf. Dillmann, *Die Bücher Numeri, Deuteronomium und Josua* (*Kurzgefasstes exegetisches Handbuch*), Leipzig, 1886, p. 418. Scholars have long been exercised by the syntactical difficulties involved in this colon. It should be recognized, however, that this phrase belongs with the preceding two cola, and forms a tricolon, 3:3:3, in which the heavenly host who surround and accompany Yahweh are described. The conception of the lesser supernatural beings as guardians is common in the ancient Near East. This motif finds expression in Deut. 32:8-9 (LXX): "When the Most High apportioned the nations, when He separated the children of men, He established the boundaries of the peoples according to the number of the *benî 'ēlîm*. But the special possession of Yahweh, is [] Jacob, the portion of his inheritance is Israel".

14. Following the LXX, καὶ πάντας οἱ ἡγιασμένοι ὑπὸ τὰς χεῖράς σου, we read *kōl qedōšîm beyādékā*. For the phrase *beyad* meaning "at the side of", cf. Zech. 4:12. Gaster's ingenious hypothesis connecting these verses with Nuzu teraphim is strained ("An Ancient Eulogy on Israel", pp. 57f.). He sets aside the opening theophany in vs. 2 without discussion, and then classifies the remainder as "an ancient eulogy on the virtues and prowess of Israel" (p. 54). On the basis of ancient Canaanite and Israelite parallels, we should expect rather a eulogy of

Yahweh, and this is true of the exordium, vs. 2-3. Whatever prowess or distinction the nation may have (e.g., the blessings of the individual tribes, and of Israel in vs. 28-29) is the gift of God, and reflects his majesty and power.

15. The shift from third to second person may go back to the poet himself. On the other hand, the Massoretic text may be a conflate of variant manuscript traditions, on the basis of early co-existing third-person and second-person recensions. Cp., for example, in vs. 28, Massoretic שמיו with Samaritan שמיך.

16. The Massoretic text is extremely difficult. The passage has long been interpreted as meaning, "They prostrated themselves at thy feet", but commentators have been unable to find a suitable root for the form תֻּכּוּ. We are tempted to read *himtakkû or the like, an infixed-*t* form from the root *mk* (*mwk* or *mkk*). The root is common to Hebrew, Aramaic, Arabic and Ugaritic, and means "to bend, to be low or humiliated". For Hebrew usage, note especially Eccl. 10:18; Job 24:24; for Ugaritic, see III AB A:17. In the Peshitta, it commonly is used to translate Hebrew *špl*. A reflexive formation with precisely this meaning is expected in the context.

In support of an infixed-*t* form, there is considerable evidence. Inscriptional data from Byblus and Moab show that the surrounding Canaanite dialects used infixed-*t* forms; this is true of Ugaritic as well. Examples of an old infixed-*t* conjugation in Hebrew are preserved in place-names, אלתקה, אשתמוע, etc., and in verbal forms, e.g., משתין, the participle of the infixed-*t* form from the root *šyn* (though generally regarded as derived from a secondary root *štn*); עתר, probably an infixed-*t* form derived from ערר, cf. Albright, "The North-Canaanite Poems of *Al'êyân Ba*^{c}*al*", *JPOS*, XIV (1934), p. 122, n. 105. In the *hištaqtal* form, השתחוה, a closely related conjugation is preserved, with almost exactly the same meaning as the proposed **himtakkû*; cf. also the forms *ištaḫaḫin* (from **ḫnḫn*) in the Amarna Letters and from Boghazkoy (called to our attention by Prof. Albright). The preformative *he* is to be expected in Hebrew, on the analogy of the Hiphil, Hithpael, and Hishtaphal. The *he* preformative is also used in Moabite with infixed-*t* forms, e.g., בהלתחמה, Mesha Stone, line 19, and הלתחם, line 32. We may be virtually certain, therefore, that the **hiqtatal* conjugation was used in tenth-century Hebrew.

Gaster derives *tukkû* from the Arabic *wk'*, long since proposed, but generally discarded by modern scholars. In order to connect *tukkû* with *wk'*, a hypothetical *wky* must first be supposed, a very questionable procedure. Further, there is no evidence for either *yk'* or *yky* in Hebrew. Gaster goes on to explain *tukkû* as an imperfect third masculine plural formed with a *t*-prefix. Such formations are quite common in Ugaritic and appear in the Amarna Letters, but their origin and precise morphology are still a matter of debate. Because of the use of this *t*-form in Hebrew and South Canaanite with subjects which are collectives or duals (as pointed out by Albright in "The Old Testament and Canaanite Language", pp. 22f.), it is safest to regard the form as a third person feminine singular, *taqtul*. It is possible that in North Canaanite, where the usage was considerably extended, the form was modified from *taqtul* to *taqtulû*; but such an analogical change is much less likely in Hebrew, where the usage died out. Massoretic *tukkû*, following the masculine plural pronoun, is hardly to be explained as such a construction.

17. Read *yiśśeʼû-m dibrôtîkā* (without change of the consonantal text), following Gaster, "An Ancient Eulogy on Israel", p. 58. Cassuto, "Il cap. 33 del Deuteronomio", p. 237, anticipated this reading in some respects.

18. Vss. 2-3 consist of three tricola, of the form 3:3:3. In spite of the fact that there are only two words in each of the last two cola of the third set, the syllable count (seven) indicates that there must be three stresses. Cp. with the first set, where each colon has only six syllables. See the general discussion of meter in footnote 1.

19. The heavenly assembly is a characteristic feature of Canaanite religious poetry. *puḫru 'elîma*, *mpḫrt 'elîma*, *banû 'el*, *dr* are terms used in Ugaritic texts to describe this assembly of the lesser gods; cf. Gordon, *Ugaritic Handbook*, II, 2:17, 25; 17:7; 107:2,3. In Hebrew we find *benê 'ēlîm*, *qedōšîm*, *qehal* and *sōd qedōšîm*, *ʿēdat 'ēl*, and *môʿēd* (Cross, "The Tabernacle", *BA*, X [1947], p. 65). Cf. Pss. 82; 29; 89:6-8; Deut. 32:8-9 (LXX); I Kings 22:19-22; Isa. 6; 14:12-15; 24:21; Jer. 23:18-22; Job, the Prologue; 15:8; 38:7. For pertinent discussions, see H. W. Robinson, "The Council of Yahweh", *JTS*, XLIV (1943), pp. 151-157; J. H. Patton, *Canaanite Parallels in the Book of Psalms*, p. 24; T. Jacobsen, "Primitive Democracy in Ancient Mesopotamia",

JNES, II (1943), pp. 159-172. The concept of the council of the gods, when taken over into Israelite poetry, is generally applied to the host of secondary supernatural beings who surround Yahweh, and prostrate themselves before him (for parallels in Ugaritic literature, cf. II D 6:49-50; I AB 1:4-10; II AB 4:20-26; V AB C:6-8; VI AB 3:23-25). This is the picture in the exordium of the Blessing of Moses, where the angelic host is portrayed encompassing Yahweh as he reveals himself in majesty and goes forth to perform mighty deeds of fearful power. Many parallels to the entire passage (vss. 2-3), its imagery and poetic motifs, may be found in the Assyro-Babylonian literature pertaining to the Akîtu festival, and in Canaanite and Hittite literature of a similar genre; for references, see Gaster, "Psalm 29", pp. 55ff. While the writers do not believe that this poem has any connection with an alleged "Enthronement Festival of Yahweh" as advocated by some scholars, there can be no doubt that the early poets of Israel were heavily influenced by the poetic imagery and modes of expression of the peoples with whom they came in contact. A striking literary parallel is found, for example, in the ritual of the temple of Anu at Uruk. The following text is taken from F. Thureau-Dangin, *Textes cunéiformes* (Louvre), Tome VI *Tablettes d'Uruk*, Paris, 1922, Pl. LXXXII, No. 43 face = *Rituels accadiens*, Paris, 1921, pp. 108f., lines 4-20:

> Prince of the gods, whose utterance holds
> sway in the constituted assembly of
> the great gods,
>
> Lord of the magnificent tiara, wondrously
> full of splendor,
>
> Great storm-rider who like a prince, awe-
> inspiring, stands upon the royal dais,
>
> To the pronouncement of thy holy mouth, the
> Igigi hearken,
>
> Together the Anunnaki proceed reverently
> before thee,
>
> At thy command the gods all together bow as
> reeds in a storm,
>
> Thy word is like a blast of the wind, making
> pasturage rich and watering-places abundant,
>
> At thy command angry gods return to their
> dwellings,
>
> All of the gods of heaven and earth with
> gifts and offerings seek thy presence.

Vss. 2-3, 26-29 are a poem, apparently drawn from a rich body of Israelite literature of similar type. In imagery, form, and vocabulary, these verses find important parallels in Ugaritic literature, and in the distinctive heroic odes of ancient Israel. There seems to be no reason, however, to posit a difference in age between the composition of this poem and the collected blessings in substantially their present form. Orthographic indications point to the same general period for both.

20. Vss. 4-5 appear to have been part of the original introduction to the collection of Blessings (later set into the framework, vss. 2-3, 26-29). The introduction has suffered badly in the process of transmission, since another part of it apparently has found its way into vs. 21b. The phrase ספון ויתא ראשי עם (vs. 21b) is doubtless to be revised on the basis of the LXX to read ויתאספון ראשי עם, as suggested by Hayman, Burkitt (cf. his note "On the Blessing of Moses", *JTS*, XXXV [1934], p. 68), and others. These words are wholly out of context in the blessing of Gad, and must inevitably be connected with the almost identical phrase in vs. 5. The succeeding bicolon, צדקת יהוה עשה ומשפטיו עם ישראל, also seems to belong to the introduction, but the exact order of the parts cannot be determined. Finally, the omission of the rubric before the blessing of Reuben suggests that additional material may have fallen out between vss. 5 and 6. It is not possible to reconstruct these verses with any degree of confidence. While a number of cola seem clear in themselves, there seems to be no way to organize them into a coherent unity, without drastic reworking of the Massoretic text.

21. Omit the *waw*, following several Samaritan manuscripts. This change improves the meter as well, cf. footnote 1 on the canons of Hebrew poetry.

22. Read *w^{e}yihyû*. The Massoretic text preserves tenth-century orthography, without indication of the final vowel. The plural form is required by syntax; note the parallels in Isa. 3:25 and 10:19. It should be pointed out that this is not the common construction, מתי מספר.

23. The most logical period for the situation described in this verse is the eleventh century, when Reuben suffered repeatedly from Ammonite incursions. The tribe had practically disappeared by the tenth century (cf. Albright, *Archaeology and the Religion of Israel*, pp. 122-123).

24. Vocalize y^e*hûdâ* or y^e*hûd*. On these forms, see Albright, "The Names 'Israel' and 'Judah' with an Excursus on the Etymology of *Tôdâh* and *Tôrâh*", *JBL*, XLVI (1927), pp. 168-178.

25. Read *tābô'an*, Qal imperfect second masculine singular with *nun energicum*. There are a number of instances of the energic form of the imperfect without pronominal suffix in the earliest Israelite poetry: e.g., Num. 23:9,19,20; 24:17; cf. Albright, "The Oracles of Balaam", *ad loc*. Other examples occur in the Song of Deborah, on which see the notes in Chapter I. The LXX rendered the word correctly by the optative with *an*, without the pronominal suffix: ἔλθοις ἄν = "mayest thou come".

26. This colon is difficult. The meaning is not clear, and the line is too short. A number of improved readings are possible. In the first place, יהו may easily have been lost by haplography following ידו. Secondly, the verb should probably be vocalized *rabbê*, the Piel imperative of *rby*, "increase, multiply". Cassuto read the verb as **rab*, an apocopated form on the analogy of *ṣaw* ("Il cap. 33 del Deuteronomio", pp. 240-241). Only the longer form, however, occurs in the Old Testament (Jud. 9:29), and it is preferable for metrical reasons as well. The line would then read, "His strength, O Yahweh, increase for him". Prof. Albright suggests the reading **yarîw*, "his seed, offspring, etc." (Acc. [*w*]*ârum*, Ugar. *yr*) in place of *yadêw*, "his hands".

27. It is to be noted that no division between Judah and the rest of Israel is stated or implied in the text. Nevertheless, Judah seems to be in serious difficulties, while Simeon to the southwest is not even mentioned. The situation described may reflect the Philistine encroachments of the twelfth-eleventh centuries.

28. In vss. 8-10, there is a complete break in style, meter and content with the rest of the poem. The relative pronoun ('*ašer*), the sign of the definite accusative ('*et*-), and the article, all suspicious in ancient poetry, occur in these lines. The poetic structure is dubious, and vs. 9 at least seems to be largely prose. Significant from the point of view of the writers is the absence of tenth-century spellings and archaic forms in this passage, while the surrounding verses abound in both. How much, if any, of vs. 8-10 belongs to the original blessing must remain a question. The passage is rejected *in toto* as a late addition by some scholars.

29. Vs. 11 swarms with archaisms and may well have been the original blessing of Levi (cp. Gen. 49:5-7).

30. Omit the *waw*, which may have been added by dittography.

31. Read probably the plural, following the LXX and Vulgate.

32. *m^eḥaṣ* is a characteristic term in old Canaanite and Hebrew poetry. It occurs frequently in the Amarna correspondence and the Ugaritic epics. Note the following examples from the Old Testament: Num. 24:8,17; Hab. 3:13; Ps. 18:39 = II Sam. 22:39; Ps. 68:22,24.

33. Read *motnê-m(i) qamîw*, following Albright, "The Old Testament and Canaanite Language", pp. 22-23. For a discussion of the enclitic *mem* between the *nomen regens* and the *nomen rectum* of a construct chain, see Albright, "The Oracles of Balaam", p. 219, n. 83. The Samaritan reflects a revision of the text in which the *mem* was omitted.

34. Omit the *waw*, which may have slipped in by dittography.

35. Read the relative pronoun, *man*, instead of the preposition which is syntactically anomalous in the present context (following Albright, "The Old Testament and Canaanite Language", pp. 23-24); on *man* in Ugaritic, see Gordon, *Ugaritic Handbook*, III, 1194. The whole phrase should be read, *man y^eqîménnû* (cp. Samaritan מן יקימנו), "whoever attacks him". Note the parallel passage (with interrogative *mî*) in Gen. 49:9 = Num. 24:9 (cf. Albright's translation in "The Oracles of Balaam", p. 225). The Massoretic text preserves tenth-century orthography.

36. Cf. the proper name ידידיה, II Sam. 12:27, and the Ugaritic appellative *ydd 'el*, "the beloved of El", 49:VI:30-31.

37. *yiškōn* is quite common in these ancient poems; cf. Gen. 49:13; Num. 23:9; Deut. 33:16, 20, 28; Ps. 68:17, 19; note also KRT A:104 = 192. Then it falls out of use, until we meet it again in very late prose. See Cross, "The Tabernacle", pp. 65ff.

38. *^cēlî hôpēp ^calêw*, "Eli hovers over him", seems to be the best reading. This follows, in part, the LXX, which reads καὶ ὁ θεὸς σκιάζει 'επ' αυτῷ ... The Samaritan and Syriac omit the first עליו, the Vulgate and several Hebrew mss. omit the second. This confusion in the versions indicates an early corruption of the text, in which the initial *^cēlî* was accidentally

altered to conform to the following ^{c}*alêw*. The divine name was first pointed out by Nyberg, although he mistakenly vocalized it ^{c}*Al*; cf. "Studien zum Religionskampf im Alten Testament", *Beiträge zur Religionswissenschaft der Religionswissenschaftlichen Gesellschaft zu Stockholm, AR*, (1938), pp. 372ff., where he notes its presence in this passage. Note other occurrences of ^{c}*Elî* in I Sam. 2:10; II Sam. 23:1. It is also found in the name *Y*^{e}*ḥaw*^{c}*ēlî* from the Samaria ostraca, and the biblical hypocoristicon ^{c}*Elî*, as pointed out by Albright in *Archaeology and the Religion of Israel*, p. 202, n. 18, and "The Old Testament and Canaanite Language", p. 31, n. 89. It probably means, "Exalted One", and must be closely connected with ^{c}*Elyon* and the Ugaritic designation of Baal, ^{c}*ly*, KRT C III:6,8.

39. *kol-hayyôm* is suspicious here, both because of the article, and for metrical reasons. It is very common in the later psalms, and may have been inserted after the loss of ^{c}*ēlî* or ^{c}*alêw* in the original text.

40. *ū-bên k*^{e}*tēpêw šākēn* is extremely difficult. For recent interpretations, see Gaster, "Deut. 33:12", *Expos. Times* 47:7 (1935), p. 334, and Phythian-Adams, "On the Date of the Blessing of Moses", pp. 158ff. Neither is particularly convincing, though Gaster is probably correct in his general analysis of the passage.

The key to the meaning of the colon is in the words *bên k*^{e}*tēpêw*. Prof. Albright, in a private communication, calls attention to a parallel usage in the Baal Epic, III AB A:14-22: *hlm . ktp . zbl ym, bn . ydm . [ṯp]ṭ . nhr ... hlm . qdqd . zbl . ym, bn .* ^{c}*nm . ṯpṭ . nhr.*

> Smite the "bosom" of Prince Sea, between the arms of Judge River,
>
> ... Smite the head of Prince Sea, between the eyes of Judge River.

We have translated *ktp*, "bosom" here because the English word "shoulder" is more restricted in meaning and does not include the front of the chest (as required by the parallelism, cp. Arabic *bai̭na yadai̭hi*, "in front"). The second bicolon clearly refers to the forehead, the first to the chest or bosom.

The phrase, *bên k*^{e}*tēpêw*, occurs only once again in the Old Testament, I Sam. 17:6. In a list of the pieces of armor which Goliath wore, the last item is וכידן נחשת בין-כ״. One suspects that the *kîdôn* here is a breast-plate (cp. Acc. *kidânu*, Arab. *kadana*), worn between the shoulders, i.e., in front, spanning the chest. Such an interpretation is doubtful, however, because *kîdôn* elsewhere is apparently a weapon like a spear or mace.

It is perhaps best to treat the passage as portraying the protective care of Yahweh for Benjamin, in close parallelism with the first colon, rather than regard it as an historical allusion to Yahweh's dwelling in a Benjaminite sanctuary (i.e., the sanctuary at Nob during the reign of Saul).

41. This blessing and the corresponding version in Gen. 49:25-26 are heavily weighted with Canaanite imagery. The blessings of fertility, the peculiar terminology, the tendency to personify natural forces (which cannot be indicated satisfactorily in translation), and especially the repetitive style, suggest a Canaanite forbear upon which both draw. For metrical parallels, see particularly II AB VI:47-54. The writers are unable to determine which form of the blessing is older. Both seem to retain preferable readings. The contents of the blessing imply Joseph's primacy among the tribes. This fact would favor, perhaps, composition at a time when Joseph dominated the confederacy. The *terminus ad quem* would be the reign of Saul.

42. *mimmeged* is equivalent to *birkôt* in Gen. 49:25-26. These ancient variants apparently arose during the period of oral transmission of the original blessing.

43. *mē*ᶜ*āl* is preferable. This reading is supported by two Hebrew mss. as well as the parallel in Gen. 49:25. It may be remarked that *ṭeth* and ᶜ*ayin* are easily confused in the early script. The source of confusion, however, may be found in a passage like Gen. 27:39.

44. *t*ᵉ*hôm* is probably personified here. Cp. Gen. 49:25; Hab. 3:10; Exod. 15:5,8; and frequent occurrences in Ugaritic.

45. Cf. Gen. 49:25, 9, 14.

46. Omit *waw*s regularly before *mimmeged*. Cp. Gen. 49:25-26 (*birkôt*). Cf. footnote 4.

47. Read probably *šamšī̌*, *metri causa*. When case endings were preserved, they generally received the accent; cf. *b*ᵉ*nô b*ᵉᶜ*ōr*, Num. 24:3, and Albright, "The Oracles of Balaam", *ad loc*. In tenth-century orthography, these case endings would not be indicated.

48. Read the plural form, "expulsions" or "yields", following the Samaritan (גרושי). The parallel term *t*^{e}*bû'ôt* is likewise in the plural. The Massoretic text preserves the older orthography; it is possible, however, that the *yodh* dropped out by haplography.

49. Read, probably, *yārē*^{a}*ḥ*, "moon" (for "month"), in parallel with *šamšî*. Omit the final *mem*, apparently a case of dittography.

50. The present text seems to be a conflate of two ancient variants. The original must have read *mimmeged* in both cola, as implied by the parallel *birkôt* in Gen. 49. An early variant, however, had *mērôš* in both cola, as shown by the LXX.

51. Vocalize, probably, *har*^{e}*rî qâdm // gib*^{c}*ôt* ^{c}*ôlām*, or the like, for metrical reasons.

52. The parallel phrases are a cliché in old Hebrew poetry, cf. Gen. 49:26; Num. 23:7; Hab. 3:6. Similar expressions occur in Ugaritic.

53. *šôk*^{e}*nî* retains the old genitive case ending (cp. Samaritan שכן). The *litterae compaginis* were preserved in archaic poetry (*metri causa*) and ancient formulas, cf. GK §90. For further discussion, see Albright, *JBL*, LXI (1942), p. 117; and "The Old Testament and Canaanite Language", pp. 18, 22. The Samaritan also preserves case endings in *rêmî*, vs. 17, and *harî*, vs. 19 (the *yodh* may have been added by dittography, however). It is reasonable to suppose that there were other case endings in the original poem, but lost in the process of transmission, cf. footnote 47. The LXX seems to translate *š*^{e}*kînâ* (ὀφθέντι), which would be natural in the third century B.C.

54. *Sinai* is probably to be read, following a number of scholars. This reading is given by some of the Samaritan mss. As already pointed out (note 3), only סנ, *sînê* would appear in tenth-century orthography. The orthography of the Massoretic text, סנה, is proper for ninth-eighth century Israel (i.e., *he* as a *mater lectionis* for final *ê*).

55. This anomalous form appears to be a conflate reading: *tābô'* followed by *t*^{e}*hî*, third person feminine singular jussives taking a collective subject; cf. footnote 16. Other examples occur in Nah. 1:5b,9 (cf. Albright, "The Old Testament and Canaanite Language", pp. 22-23); Hab. 3:9 (cf. Albright, "The Psalm of Habakkuk"); Ps. 68:3; cf. also Gaster, "An Ancient

Eulogy on Israel", p. 57, n. 8. *t^e hî* is preferable to *tābô'* (an ancient variant), on the basis of the parallel in Gen. 49:26, תהיין, which should be vocalized **tihyan(na)* or the like (a feminine singular with energic *nun*, also taking a collective subject); on the form, see footnote 25. תה, *t^e hî*, is an example of archaic spelling preserved in the Massoretic text.

56. This expression is characteristic of Ugaritic and ancient Israelite poetry. Cf. Gen. 49:26; Num. 24:17 (as emended according to the Samaritan); Deut. 33:20; Ps. 68:22.

57. The Samaritan (supported by the LXX, Vulgate, and Peshitta) reads simply שור, thus preserving archaic orthography (without indication of the final vowel, *ô*). The Massoretic text, however, has the correct vocalization, and reflects a later revision of the spelling.

58. The *waw* may have slipped in by dittography.

59. Vocalize *rêmî*, with the Samaritan (ראמי), for metrical reasons. The word also occurs frequently in archaic poetry. Cf. Ps. 22:22; 29:6; Num. 23:22; 24:8; and it is common in the Ras Shamrah texts.

60. Read possibly *yidḥê*, from the root *dḥy*, "to push violently, thrust", and perhaps "gore". This emendation involves a simple metathesis of the second and third letters. C. J. Ball, "The Blessing of Moses", *Proceedings of the Society of Biblical Archaeology*, 1896, *ad loc.*, reads *wayyaddaḥ*, from *ndḥ*, a kindred root. However, he supplies a conjunction which would be out of place in this poetry, and the root *dḥy* seems preferable on the basis of recorded usage. Albright, "The Psalm of Habakkuk", finds a parallel reading in Hab. 3:4; cf. also I AB VI:17,18.

61. The LXX reads the singular here, ἄκρου γῆς, indicating that in the underlying Hebrew text, there was no *yodh* marking the construct plural form. In early orthography, both singular and construct plural would have been written אפס.

62. Omit the *waw*, following the Samaritan, LXX, Vulgate, and Peshitta. The *waw* at the beginning of the second colon should likewise be omitted, cf. footnote 4. המ is probably to be translated "lo, behold" = Ugaritic *hm*. The vocalization is uncertain.

63. This couplet is an excellent example of symmetry in the structure of old Hebrew poetry. Note the balanced expressions: *rib^e bôt 'eprêm // 'alpî m^e naššê* (by syllabic count, 3 2 // 2 3). See footnote 1.

64. This colon lacks a stress, and a parallel to *ś*^{e}*maḥ* is required. Read perhaps either שש יששכר באהלכ or ישש יששכר באהלו. *śyś* occurs regularly in parallelism with *śmḥ*, and could easily have been lost by haplography, since its consonants are duplicated in the following word: ⌈י⌉שש יששכר. This emendation is made more attractive by a possible play on words, examples of which are common in the tribal blessings (Gen. 49, *passim*).

65. Parts of vs. 19 are quite clear, but the precise meaning of the two bicola remains obscure. Vs. 19a has generally been interpreted as a reference to some North Israelite cult. The most extreme treatment of the historical implications of this verse is that of O. Eissfeldt, "Der Gott des Tabor und seine Verbreitung", *Archiv für Religionswissenschaft*, XXXI Heft 1/2, pp. 14-41. Whether or not his conclusions about a Tabor cult are warranted, it is difficult to accept such an interpretation of these words. The usual translation, "They shall call the people unto the mountain", is syntactically improbable. It is possible to read *hérâ* (with *he* directive, spelled *hr*[*h*] in tenth-century orthography, cf. footnote 75). Cp., however, Samaritan הרי. That the text is in disarray is amply indicated by the LXX.

66. Massoretic *marḥîb* is suspicious as the only instance in which the blessing is applied to Yahweh instead of the tribe. Read rather, in all probability, *merḥab* or *merḥ*^{a}*bî gād*, "the broad land(s) of Gad". Gad was the strongest tribe on the table-land east of the Jordan.

67. As generally recognized, we must insert *gād* here, for metrical reasons. What is not generally recognized is that a haplography of considerable length is involved; there is no connection between the first colon and those which follow, however the first words are interpreted.

68. Vocalize *lābî'* or *lébe'* (cf. Albright, "The Oracles of Balaam", p. 218, n. 75), "lioness".

69. Omit the *waw*, with the Samaritan.

70. Read *w*^{e}*yir'ê*, present tense, according to the context (see footnote 71). Tenth-century spelling would permit either vocalization of the verb.

71. The best suggestion is to read **kîššōm*, a contraction from *kî yiššom*, "for he pants after". The root *nšm* occurs in Hebrew only in Isa. 42:14. However, the substantive *n*^{e}*šāmâ*,

"breath", which is quite common, and Arabic *nasama* establish its meaning beyond doubt, as "to pant" or "to breathe heavily". The contraction is indicated by metrical considerations (the second colon would otherwise be considerably longer than the first); and the present text could easily be explained on the basis of such a contraction. It may be noted in passing that the syncope of *yodh* between *i* vowels (**iyi* > *î*) is strictly in accord with Hebrew phonetic laws. There can be no doubt that contractions occurred in Hebrew poetry (*metri causa*), just as they do in the poetry of other languages.

72. *mᵉḥôqēq* also occurs in Gen. 49:10 and Jud. 5:14; this is another instance of the closely related vocabulary of ancient Israelite poems.

73. For a discussion of vs. 21b, see footnote 20.

74. Contrary to the usual view, there is no natural association between Dan and Bashan. Prof. Albright has suggested to the writers the rendering *bāšān* = serpent, viper; cp. Proto-Sinaitic and Ugaritic *bṯn*, "serpent", and Arabic *bṯn*, "viper". Hebrew *péten* is possibly a very early Aramaic loanword, ultimately derived from the same root. We read *mibbāšān* for metrical reasons; in any case, the article is not expected in early Hebrew poetry. *bāšān* may have a similar meaning ("sea-dragon?") in Ps. 68:23; cf. also, Ugaritic 67:I:1. It is interesting to note that in Gen. 49:17, Dan is described as a viper.

75. The meaning is obscure. "West and South" seems to be the best interpretation at present. The Massoretic text has ים, as against Samaritan ימה. This implies that the *he* directive had lost consonantal force by the tenth century, and therefore was not indicated in the orthography. The evidence, however, is much too uncertain to warrant any general conclusion.

76. Read *yîraš*, "he will inherit", following the Samaritan יירש (supported by the LXX, Vulgate, and Peshitta). Massoretic *yᵉrāšâ* is apparently a conflate reading: *yîraš*, imperfect or jussive, and *rᵉšâ*, emphatic imperative.

77. Read, probably, *yihyê*. The Massoretic text preserves the early orthography.

78. Omit the *waw*, which may have slipped in by dittography.

79. Read *raglêw*, "his feet", following the Samaritan.

80. Vs. 25 is difficult both as to meaning and meter. Of interest is *dob'ékā*, "thy strength" (but the Samaritan reads

רביך), which is to be compared with Ugaritic *db'atk* (so Ginsberg and Gordon), IV AB II:21-22: *qrn . db'atk . btlt ᶜnt . qrn db'atk*, "the horns of thy strength, O virgin Anat, the horns of thy strength".

81. We adopt, for metrical reasons, Cassuto's suggestion, *'ên ['ēl] kᵉ'ēl yᵉšūrûn*, "Il cap. 33 del Deuteronomio", pp. 249-250. Compare Ugaritic V AB E:40-41 = II AB IV:43ff.: *'alyn . bᶜl . ṯpṭn* (41) *'en . dᶜlnh.*

82. Read *rôkēb šāmêm bᵉᶜuzzô rôkēb bᵉgē'ûtô šᵉḥāqîm*; cf. Cross and Freedman, "A Note on Deuteronomy 33:26", *BASOR* #108 (1947), pp. 6-7. On the reading *gē'ûtô*, note the Samaritan גאתו. On the omission of the *waw* at the beginning of the second colon, see footnote 4. From the metrical standpoint, the second colon is a little long; it actually may have sounded something like this: *rôkēbᵉgē'ûtô šᵉḥāqîm*. The merging of the two *b* sounds in speech may underlie the resulting corruption of the text. Cp. חיהוה, Lachish Letter III:9; ביטב, Bir RKB Inscr., line 16; etc.

83. Read *mᵉᶜônô*, "his place of refuge". On the orthography, see footnote 8. The verse is awkwardly placed here; the antecedent is Jacob-Israel. For this reason, it is perhaps preferable to transpose the bicolon to the end of vs. 28. See footnotes 84 and 88.

84. Inserting a *waw*, we read *mittaḥtêw*, "under him". Since this is an analogical formation, it is possible that a form **taḥtô* also existed. In that case, no change in the Massoretic text would be necessary. Gaster's reconstruction of this bicolon ("An Ancient Eulogy on Israel", pp. 60-61), is ingenious, but diverges too far from Israelite religious concepts to permit ready acceptance. Cp. Bertholet's reconstruction, *Deuteronomium*, pp. 103-104, which in some respects is superior. Gordis' rendition ("The Text and Meaning of Deuteronomy 33:27") is syntactically inadmissible, and no improvement on the Massoretic text. H. L. Ginsberg's suggestion, *BASOR* #110 (1948), while attractive, takes too many liberties with the text.

85. *ᶜôlām*, "the Eternal One". A divine name is definitely expected after *zᵉrōᶜôt*, to parallel *'ᵉlōhî qēdem*. *ᶜOlam* as a divine appellative is well known, cf. Albright, *From the Stone Age to Christianity*, 2nd ed., Baltimore, 1946, p. 188, and Baudissin, *Adonis und Esmun*, Leipzig, 1911, pp. 486ff. Baudissin

discusses the use of *El* ᶜ*Olam* and ᶜ*Olam* alone as Hebrew appellatives (cp., for example, El Shaddai and Shaddai, El ᶜElyon and ᶜElyon). He also calls attention to Phoenician Οὐλωμός.

86. The second half of the line is defective. Meek (in *The Bible, An American Translation*) reads "the Amorite" instead of *wayyômer*, which may be correct (cf. Amos 2:9). However, a stress is still missing, and any emendation must remain a conjecture.

87. Read ᶜ*ān*, following Cassuto, "Il cap. 33 del Deuteronomio", pp. 249-250. Budde, *Der Segen Mose's*, pp. 16-17, first recognized the verbal root, and explained the meaning of the passage. Von Hoonacker, "La bénédiction de Moïse", *Le Muséon*, XLII (1929), p. 59, called attention to the excellent parallel in Isa. 13:21,22, but vocalized *yā*ᶜ*ûn*. See also Gaster, "An Ancient Eulogy on Israel", pp. 61-62.

88. Read ᶜ*al* with the Samaritan, as generally recognized. Read also, *'arṣô*, "his land", in parallel with שמיו, "his heavens". The suffix would not have been indicated in early orthography.

89. Cf. *trṯ* in Ugaritic, II Aqht VI:7.

90. As already indicated (footnote 1), the structure of these bicola is 2:2.2:2. The first colon is a hypermetrical conflate of two early variants: *'ašrêkā y*ᵉ*śir'ēl* and *y*ᵉ*śir'ēl mî-kāmôkā*.

91. Read *māginnô* ᶜ*ezrêkā ḥarbô gē'ûtêkā*. We owe the reading, in part, to Ginsberg, *BASOR* #110. The third person suffix would not be indicated in tenth-century orthography. The relative pronoun in such constructions is generally omitted in early poetry. *'a*ˇ*šer* in the second colon may be a case of dittography, cf. Cassuto, "Il cap. 33 del Deuteronomio", p. 251. It is to be omitted, in any case, for metrical reasons.

92. Omit the *waw*, cf. footnote 4. On *yikkāḥ*ᵃ*šû*, cp. Ps. 18:45 and II Sam. 22:45. All three forms have approximately the same meaning. They express the cringing fear and feigned obeisance of the conquered.

93. The Samaritan text, במתמ, preserves tenth-century spelling, while the Massoretic text gives the archaic poetic vocalization of the suffix. Read ᶜ*al-bmôtîmô*, for metrical reasons; cf. Albright, "The Earliest Forms of Hebrew Verse", p. 85, n. 4. The LXX reads "neck" or "back of neck", for this word.

Old Testament parallels are to be found in Deut. 32:13; Hab. 3:19; Ps. 18:34. Cf. Gaster, "An Ancient Eulogy on Israel", p. 62.

CHAPTER V

A ROYAL SONG OF THANKSGIVING

II SAMUEL 22 = PSALM 18

CHAPTER V

A ROYAL SONG OF THANKSGIVING
II SAMUEL 22 = PSALM 18[a]

The importance of this poem for the study of textual transmission can scarcely be overemphasized. No other ancient piece of comparable length appears in parallel texts in the Old Testament. Scholars have recognized that a long complex history lies behind the present Massoretic recensions of the Psalm. In their earlier written form, II Samuel 22 and Psalm 18 represented divergent traditions, with a maximum number of variant readings. Subsequent developments involved the interaction of the texts upon each other, and a strong tendency toward harmonization. This process, however, was never completed, and the result consists of the mixed texts which we have.[b] The variant and conflate readings, which are still preserved in considerable number, strikingly illustrate both processes in the textual history of the Psalm.[c]

Significant also are the orthographic peculiarities of the texts. As pointed out by Hitzig, Delitzsch and Kittel, among others, II Sam. 22 is written more defectively (i.e., with fewer *matres lectiones*) than Psalm 18. Both texts have been revised and modernized considerably in the course of transmission[d], but II Sam. 22 preserves a number of archaic readings which point to a minimal date in the ninth-eighth centuries B.C. for the written composition of the poem. These old spellings reflect a text written in the dialect of Israel, the Northern Kingdom, and which must therefore antedate the destruction of Samaria (722/1 B.C.), i.e., at a time before normative Israelite written sources were superseded by a shift to standard Judahite channels.

It is now known that the diphthongs *ay* and *aw* were regularly contracted in Israelite, as in Phoenician, but were preserved in Judahite until the Exile or later. In Israelite, the contracted diphthongs were treated as vowels, and not indicated in the orthography[e]; in Judahite, on the other hand, the consonantal element in the diphthong was represented (by *waw* or *yodh*).[f] The generally defective spelling of II Sam. 22 suggests a preexilic date.[g] In addition, there are eleven cases of words containing, originally, the diphthong *aw*. Of these, seven are written according to Israelite practice, without the *waw*.[h] The same words in Psalm 18 are spelled in accordance with Judahite practice (i.e., with the *waw*) which, with some modifications, became standard in post-exilic times.[i]

The presence of such orthographic archaisms in II Sam. 22 is remarkable. There is now considerable evidence to show that biblical orthography passed through a late phase of extremely full writing.[j] It is to be assumed that biblical scholars of the Rabbinic period revised these texts on the basis of much older witnesses available to them, and thus produced the relatively moderate orthography of the delivered text (i.e., with fewer *matres lectionis*). The preservation, or perhaps restoration, of archaic orthography was apparently the result of such a procedure. It should be emphasized, nevertheless, that in the light of the complex history of the transmission of the Hebrew text, individual cases of archaic spelling do not constitute sufficient evidence for the dating of biblical passages.[k] What is required is an accumulation of instances in a single section; even then, collateral linguistic evidence is highly desirable.[l]

Comparison of the two texts is invaluable for the identification of archaic linguistic phenomena. Noteworthy examples are to be found in the description of the theophany in vss. 8-16. The use of the preposition ב meaning, "from", in vs. 14 (Psalm 18) and 16 (II Sam. 22), is confirmed by the parallel passages where מ(ן) appears.[m] Similarly, the presence of the archaic enclitic particle *m(i)* in Ps. 18:16, *'^{a}pīqê-m yām*, is established by comparison with the parallel in II Sam. 22:16, *'^{a}pīqê yām*.[n]

The texts under consideration also provide valuable evidence for historical development in the use of the conjunction "and" (*waw*) at the beginning of cola.[o] An examination of the material shows that the use of the conjunction follows no determinable set of rules. Rather, they seem to be distributed at random, haphazardly inserted in one text, omitted in the other. A summary of the evidence follows. Comparing the two Hebrew texts, we find for II Samuel 22, of a total of 106 cola, 47 begin with the conjunction; for Psalm 18, of a total of 107 cola, 47 begin with the conjunction.[p] The two texts differ, however, in 16 instances. There are eight cases in which Psalm 18 reads the conjunction, while II Sam. 22 omits it; in the other eight cases, the reverse is true.[q] The data of the versions simply add to the general confusion. In the LXX of II Sam. 22, 54 cola are introduced by *καί*; there are nine instances of divergence from the Massoretic text of II Sam. 22. In the LXX of Psalm 18, 53 cola are introduced by *καί*; there are six cases of divergence from the Massoretic text of Psalm 18.[r] In the Vulgate of II Sam. 22, 41 cola begin with the conjunction; there are 18 instances in which the Vulgate diverges from the Massoretic text of II Sam. 22. In the Vulgate of Psalm 18 (following Lagarde's critical edition), 40 cola begin with the conjunction; there are nine cases of divergence from the Massoretic text of Psalm 18.[s] In the Peshitta of II Sam. 22, 66 cola begin with the conjunction; there are 38 cases of divergence from the Massoretic text of II Samuel. In the Peshitta of Psalm 18, 60 cola begin with the conjunction; there are 34 cases of divergence from the Massoretic text of Psalm 18.[t] It may be observed that the Peshitta of II Samuel has been harmonized to a considerable extent with that of Psalm 18. In all, the use of the conjunction is attested by the Hebrew texts and versions without exception, for only 22 cola.[u]

In any given case, therefore, it would be very difficult to determine whether the conjunction were to be read or not. Since, however, the conjunction is used very sparingly in Ugaritic as well as in the earliest Hebrew poetry, to introduce cola, it is to be supposed that in the more original form of the poem, very few cola appeared with the conjunction.[v] In the transmission of the text, there was a tendency to insert the conjunction at the beginning of cola. A comparison of the Hebrew texts and the different versions indicates several different stages in this development. Efforts apparently were made at various times to revise the texts on the basis of older manuscript tradition, and eliminate some of the superfluous conjunctions in the poem.[w]

The evidence for the use of the conjunction in these texts also has important bearing upon the occurrence of the imperfect with and without the so-called *waw* consecutive in early Hebrew poetry. C. H. Gordon has pointed out that the imperfect of the verb (in particular the "jussive" form) is used frequently to express the past tense; in addition, there is a regular sequence of tenses in Ugaritic (i.e., the intermingling of perfect forms with the imperfect), in which, however, the conjunction is not always or even generally used.[x] A number of clear instances of precisely the same phenomenon occur in Exodus 15, one of the earliest Hebrew poems extant.[y] In the present poem as well, there are a number of instances of the imperfect used to express past time. In seven cases of this sort, the verb appears with *waw* consecutive in one text, without it in the other (cp. vss. 7, 12,14,16,39 bis, 44).[z]

This phenomenon has been misunderstood by a number of scholars. Buttenwieser maintains that many of these imperfects must be regarded as jussives, and interprets the Psalm as an entreaty or prayer for help and victory in the future.[aa] Löhr supposes that the series of imperfects in the latter part of the Psalm (vss. 32-50) indicate prophetic expectation. Others, like Briggs, suppose that if the imperfect is to be regarded as referring to past time, then it must be preceded by the *waw* consecutive. It can no longer be doubted, however, that the imperfect form of the verb was the common, generally-used verb form in old Israelite poetry, as in old Canaanite poetry, and that its time aspect was determined by the context, not the presence or absence of the conjunction.

The Davidic authorship of II Sam. 22 = Psalm 18 was commonly accepted by the older scholars of the nineteenth century, including Ewald, Hitzig and Delitzsch, among others. With some reservations as to the authorship, the early date for the Psalm is still held by some modern scholars (e.g., Briggs, omitting glosses, and Albright). Scholars like Kittel, Gunkel and Driver, while denying a tenth-century date, nevertheless place the poem in pre-exilic times.[bb] Many modern scholars follow Duhm, Spoer, Cheyne, and others in dating the Psalm after the exile, some even as late as the Maccabaean Era.[cc] Still others, like Hans Schmidt, divide the Psalm into a number of sections, and assign the different parts to different periods.

The present writers hold that the poem as a whole was written down in substantially its present form not later than the ninth-eighth centuries B.C. A number of considerations point to this conclusion. The orthographic evidence strongly implies that the poem was written before the fall of Samaria. The linguistic archaisms discussed above occur only in the oldest Hebrew and Canaanite literature. The language and style of the theophany (vs. 8-16) derive from ancient Canaanite sources, having many contacts with the Ugaritic epics. The literary associations with Exod. 15, Hab. 3[dd], Deut. 32 and 33, Micah 7, and Psalm 144, point to a relatively early date for the composition of the Psalm. Finally, the inclusion of the poem in II Samuel, along with the "Last Words of David" (itself a very archaic poem) shows that an old tradition associated the Psalm with the early monarchy. A tenth-century date for the poem is not at all improbable.

The unity of the Psalm frequently has been called into question. Most scholars find a major dividing point at vs. 32; however, uncertainty as to the meaning of vs. 30 and the authenticity of vs. 31 cause some disagreement.

It seems clear that the author of the Psalm drew on a number of older sources. The theophany in vss. 8-16 with its Canaanite associations is of a piece with the ancient poetry of Israel, belonging to the period of the Judges and early monarchy. Similarly in vss. 26-27, an old gnomic couplet with sing-song rhythm and anthropopathic conceptions is apparently quoted by the psalmist. The first main section, vss. 2-7, 17-31 (into which the theophany fits very smoothly it is to be noted) expresses the praise and thanksgiving of the poet for deliverance from his desperate trouble. The second main part, vss. 32-50, seems to apply specifically to a leader or king who exalts Yahweh for his powerful aid in battle. A significant element and familiar motif in this victory song is the description of the arming of the king, and the conquest of his enemies. It remains a question as to whether the psalm is an amalgamation of two or more independent odes, or a single poem sharply divided into separate parts.

Notes to the Introduction

a. This study has developed out of a seminar on the Psalm conducted by Prof. Albright at the Johns Hopkins University. We are indebted to Prof. Albright for many valuable suggestions.

b. Scribal errors in the transmission of each text must be recognized. Evidence for inner corruptions in the Samuel and Psalms versions will be found in the notes to the text.

c. In the first four verses, we find two different but parallel introductions to the ancient hymn (cf. note 2 to the text). II Sam. 22 and Psalm 18 are conflate texts preserving readings from both introductory passages. Efforts were made to harmonize the two texts, with the result that the metrical form and poetic parallelism have almost completely disappeared. Other striking examples of conflation are to be found in vss. 7 (see note 13 to the text), 12-13 (notes 31-33), 28, 29, 38, 39, 49. In certain cases, the variants are preserved in the different texts, in others as conflate readings side by side in the same recension.

d. In the course of transmission, both texts have undergone general grammatical and orthographic revision. This was an inevitable process in the transmission of literature in the ancient Near East (as is attested by succeeding editions of the same literary document; this is true of Accadian and Egyptian literary works, as well as others). The Psalms rendition, as might be expected, has been revised more completely than that of II Samuel.

e. There is no evidence whatsoever for the use of *matres lectionis* in a medial position in the Northern dialect (at least until the fall of Samaria), or the Southern dialect (the first traces of such usage come from the latest pre-exilic period). Final vowel sounds, however, were indicated in Hebrew after the tenth century B.C., by the appropriate vowel letter: *he*, *waw*, or *yodh*.

f. The use of *internal matres lectionis* developed in part as a result of the contraction of internal diphthongs in the exilic or post-exilic period. At the same time, historical spelling preserved the *waw* and *yodh* of the former diphthongs; these thus became vowel letters representing respectively *ô* and *ê*. For a detailed discussion of Hebrew orthography, see the forthcoming study by Cross and Freedman.

g. In addition, there seems to be at least one case in which *he* appears as the third person masculine singular pronominal suffix (cf. note 34 to the text). This spelling is peculiar to the pre-exilic period.

h. Another possible case occurs in vs. 46. יבלו is perhaps to be vocalized *yôbilū*.

i. While it is possible that a few archaic spellings might be introduced coincidentally through scribal error, the accumulation of such spellings in II Sam. 22 tends to rule out that possibility.

j. Different stages in the later development of Hebrew orthography may be traced in the newly discovered documents of the Maccabaean Age (the [c]Ain Feshkha manuscripts including the two Isaiah scrolls, the Habakkuk Commentary, etc.) Two different orthographic traditions seem to be represented in these manuscripts: thoroughly *plene* spelling as in the complete Isaiah scroll, and relatively moderate use of *matres lectionis* as reported in the Isaiah fragment from the Hebrew University. The latter resembles the orthography of the Massoretic text. Other sources for the history of Hebrew orthography are the extant transcriptions from the second column of the Hexapla and Jerome's writings; various early (first millennium of this era) Hebrew manuscripts, with Palestinian punctuation, collected by P. Kahle in *Masoreten des Westens*, Stuttgart, 1927.

k. This is particularly true of prose passages, where orthographic revision was carried out most consistently. Such archaisms as occur may best be explained as due to scribal error, coincidence, or misinterpretation. For all practical purposes, the use of spelling as an objective criterion for dating is limited to poetic passages.

l. There are a number of possible tenth-century spellings in the text of the poem (these are indicated in the notes to the text). It may be questioned, however, whether these are sufficient to demonstrate the early date of the composition of the poem. Cf. notes 32, 64, 99.

m. In each case, the original *b* has been replaced by the more commonly used *min* following later usage. This is a clear example of editorial revision in process. See note 20.

n. The omission of the *mem* is another instance of editorial revision, cf. note 12.

o. In the chart at the end of this study, the evidence for the presence or absence of the conjunction at the beginning of cola is given, including the readings of the two Hebrew texts and the principal versions (beginning at vs. 4, since vs. 2-3 are not easily divided into cola). Cola divisions follow the Massoretic text.

p. Vss. 4-51 inclusive.

q. A number of these divergences involve verbs in the *yqtl* form, in one text following *waw* consecutive, in the other, not.

r. These figures are based on the readings in Codex Vaticanus; variants are taken from the apparatus in *The Old Testament in Greek*, II:1 Cambridge, 1927. If these are taken into consideration, then the number of divergences from the Massoretic text is considerably increased. For details, see the chart.

s. For variant readings, see the chart. These are derived from Lagarde's *Psalterium iuxta Hebraeos Hieronymi*, Leipzig, 1874, for Psalm 18, and from C. Vercellone's *Variae Lectiones Vulgatae Latinae Bibliorum*, II, Rome, 1864, for II Samuel.

t. For the Peshitta of Psalm 18, the text of the Codex Ambrosianus, as printed in Nestle's *Psalterium Tetraglottum*,

Tübingen, 1879, has been followed; variant readings have been taken from the critical edition by W. E. Barnes, *The Peshitta Psalter*, Cambridge, 1904.

u. It might be supposed that the use of the conjunction in the versions has been influenced to some extent by the nature of the translation language. Thus for both texts, the LXX, Vulgate and Peshitta have approximately the same number of conjunctions, though differing markedly from each other. Thus, the conjunction appears much more frequently in the Peshitta than in the Vulgate, while the total for the LXX agrees more nearly with the Massoretic text. Generalizations about the versions drawn from this evidence, however, are risky. Although the conjunction appears frequently in the Peshitta in cola where the Hebrew text does not have it, there are, nevertheless, a considerable number of cases where the conjunction appears in the Massoretic text and is omitted in the Peshitta (for details, see the chart). By the same token, there seems to be a tendency in the Vulgate to omit the conjunction at the beginning of cola, disagreeing with the Massoretic text in a number of cases. Nevertheless, there are too many cases of the reverse to warrant a conclusion as to the characteristic usage of the Latin text.

Another, perhaps more probable, explanation is that the versions reproduce with considerable fidelity their Hebrew *Vorlagen* with respect to the use of the conjunction. The wide variation in the versions would then arise from extensive differences in the Hebrew manuscripts of the different periods.

v. The victory ode in Exod. 15 is a striking case in point. In this very ancient poem, the text of which has been preserved with remarkable accuracy, the conjunction at the beginning of cola hardly appears at all. Compare Gordon's remarks on Psalm 68, *Ugaritic Handbook*, I, §14.2 (p. 114).

w. The tendency to increase the number of conjunctions reached its climax apparently in the Maccabaean age; in the following centuries, a reaction set it (as seen in the Vulgate and in the present Massoretic text). Cf. note 20.

x. Cf. Gordon, *Ugaritic Handbook*, I, §9.7.

y. Note examples in vs. 5, 12, 14, 15. For detailed discussion, see the chapter on Exod. 15.

z. Note in addition the case in vs. 41.

aa. M. Buttenwieser, *The Psalms*, Chicago, 1938, pp. 456ff.

bb. R. Kittel, *Die Psalmen* (*Kommentar zum Alten Testament*), Leipzig, 1922, *ad loc.*, dates the theophany in vss. 8-16 in the tenth century or even earlier.

cc. B. Duhm, *Die Psalmen*, Tübingen, 1922, dates the psalm in the period of Alexander Jannaeus.

dd. Parts of the Psalm of Habakkuk are extremely archaic, as has been shown by Prof. Albright; see his forthcoming study in the T. H. Robinson Anniversary volume.

II Samuel 22 = Psalm 18[1]

English	Verse	Hebrew	Meter
....		[2]___________	
The breakers of Death encompassed me,	5	[3]אפפני משברי[4] מת[5]	3
The torrents of Belial overwhelmed me,		נחלי בליעל[6] יבעתני	3
The cords of Sheol surrounded me,	6	חבלי שאל סבבני[7]	3
The traps of Death confronted me.		קדמני[8] מקשי מת	3
When I was in trouble, I called, "Yahweh",	7	בצר-לי אקרא יהוה	3
And unto my God I cried for help.		ואל אלהי אשוע[9]	3
From his palace he heard my voice,		[10]ישמע מהכלה[11] קלי	3
My cry {reached his ears / reached him}		⸢ו⸣שועתי[12] {תבא באזנו / לפנו תבא}[13]	3
The earth did quake and shake,	8	[14]⸢ו⸣תגעש ותרעש[15] ⸢ו⸣ארץ[16]	3
The foundations of the hills shuddered.		מסדי הרם[17] ירגזו	3
....		[18]___________	
Smoke rose from his nostrils	9	[19]עלה עשן באפו[20]	3
And fire from his mouth, devouring,		ראש מפ⸢ה⸣ו[21] תאכל	3
Coals flamed forth from him.		גחלם בערו ממנו	3
He spread apart the heavens and descended,	10	[22]⸢ו⸣[23]יטה[24]ב שמם וירד	3
A storm-cloud under his feet.		[25]⸢ו⸣ערפל תחת רגלו	3
He rode upon the Cherubim,	11	[26]⸢ו⸣ירכב על[27] כרב<ם>[28]	3
He flew upon the wings of of the wind,		{⸢ו⸣ידאה / ⸢ו⸣יעף}[29] על כנפי רח	3

He set darkness round about him,	12	[30]ישת חשך[31] סבבתו	3
His pavilion is the rain-cloud.		[32]סכתה חשרת[33] מם	3
{There were cloud-banks before him / Before him the clouds raced by,}	13	{עבי שחקם נגדה / נגדה עבם עברו}[34]	3
Hail and thunderbolts.		ברד וגחלי אש	3
From the heavens Yahweh thundered,	14	ירעם[35] בשמם יהוה	3
And Elyon gave forth his voice.		ועלין יתן קלה[36]	3
He shot forth arrows and scattered them,	15	[37]⌜ר⌝ישלח חצם[38] ויפצם	3
Lightning he flashed and discomfited them.		⌜י⌝ברקם<ברק>[39] ויהמם	3
The sources of the sea were exposed,	16	[40]⌜ר⌝יראו אפק-ם[41] ים	3
The foundations of the world were laid bare,		יגלו מסדת תבל	3
At thine angry shout, O Yahweh,		[42]בגערתכה יהוה	3
At the blast of thy nostrils.		מנשמת רח אפכה[43]	3
He stretched forth his hand from on high,	17	ישלח <ידה>[44] ממרם[45] [ ][46]	3
He drew me from the deep waters.		ימשני ממם רבם	3
He rescued me from my enemies when they were too strong,	18	יצלני[47] מאיבי <כי[48]> ⌜עז⌝	3
From my foes when they were mightier than I.		משנאי כי אמצו ממני	3

They attacked me in the day of my disaster	19	יקדמני[49] בים אדי	3
But Yahweh became my stay.		ויהי יהוה[50] משען לי	3
He brought me out into a place of freedom,	20	[51]⌜ו⌝יצאני למרחב	3
He liberated me because he was pleased with me.		יהלצני כי חפץ בי	3
Yahweh rewarded me according to my righteousness,	21	יגמלני יהוה כצדקי[52]	3
According to my innocence he repaid me.		כבר ידי ישב לי	3
For I have kept the ways of Yahweh	22	כי שמרתי דרכי יהוה	3
And I have not rebelled against my God.		ולא ⌜פ⌝שעתי מאלהי[53]	3
For all his judgments are before me,	23	כי כל-משפטו[54] לנגדי	3
His statutes I have not put aside from me.		⌜ו⌝חקתו לא-אסר ⌜מ⌝מני[55]	3
I have been straightforward with him,	24	[56]⌜ו⌝אהיה[57] תמם עמה	3
I have guarded myself from iniquity.		⌜ו⌝אשתמר מעוני[58]	3
....		[59]___________	
With the faithful thou art faithful,	26	עם-חסד תתחסד	2
With the straight-forward thou art straight-forward,		עם[60][]-תמם תתמם	2
With the pure in heart thou art pure,	27	עם-נבר תתברר	2
But with the crooked thou art perverse.		ועם-עקש תתפתל[61]	2

Thou wilt deliver a lowly people,	28	⌜[62]אתה עם עני תשע	3
{But haughty eyes / But the haughty-eyed} thou dost humble.		{רענם רמת / רענים רמת} [63]תשפל	3
For thou art my {light / lamp} O Yahweh	29	כי אתה {ארי / נרי}[64] יהוה	3
My God illumines my darkness.		אלהי[65] יגה חשכי	3
....		[66]--------------	
This is the God whose way is perfect;	31	[67]האל תמם דרכה	3
The word of Yahweh is tested;		אמרת יהוה צרפה	3
He is a shield to those who trust in him.		מגן הא[68] ל⌜חסם בה	

Who is God except Yahweh?	32	⌜[69]מי אל מבלעדי יהוה	3
Who is the Rock but our God?		⌜[70]מי צר זלתי[71] אלהנו	3
Yahweh is my fortress and my army,	33	<יהוה>[72] מעזי[73] וחילי[74] [][75]	3
Who makes my feet like does,	34	משוה רגלי[76] כאילת	3
Who makes me stand upon the back of Death.		על במתי[77] <מת>[78] יעמדני	3
Who trained my hands for the onslaught,	35a	מלמד ידי <לקרב>[79]	3
{My fingers for battle; / For battle, my arms;}		{ואצבעתי למלחמה / למלחמה [] זרעתי}	3
Thou hast given me thy shield of victory	36a	⌜[80]תתן-לי מגן ישעכה	3
Together with the javelin and the bow of bronze.	35b	וחנית[81] וקשת נחשה	3
Thy right hand upholds me,	36b	[82]ימנכה תסעדני	
And thy favor makes me great.		וענתכה[83] תרבני	

English	Verse	Hebrew	
Thou hast given me long-striding legs,	37	תרחב צעדי תחתני[84]	3
And my ankles do not give way.		ולא מעדו קרסלי	3
I pursue my enemies, {I destroy them / I overtake them}	38	ארדף[85] איבי ר⌝{אשמדם / אשגם}[86]	3
I do not turn back until I have annihilated them.		י⌝לא אשב עד[87] כלתם	3
{I annihilate them and they rise no more, / I smash them so that they cannot rise,}	39	[88]{אכלם ולא יקמן[89] / אמחצם ולא יכלו קם}	3
They fall beneath my feet.		יפלו תחת רגלי	3
Thou hast girded me with might for battle,	40	[90]ר⌝תזרני חל למלחמה	3
Thou hast brought down my adversaries beneath me,		תכרע קמי תחתני	3
Thou hast given me the neck of my enemies.	41a	ר⌝איבי נתתה[91] לי ערף[92]	3
My foes, I exterminate them,	41b	[93]משנאי אצמתם	3
I pulverize them like the dust of the earth,	43	י⌝אשחקם כעפר ארץ[94]	3
As the dirt of the streets I crush them.		כטט חצת אדקם[95]	3
They cried out but there was no savior,	42	ישועו ואן משע[96]	3
Unto Yahweh, but he answered them not.		אל[97] יהוה ולא ענם	3
Thou hast delivered me from the strife of the people,	44	[98]תפלטני מרבי עמי[99]	3
Thou hast guarded me..........		תשמרני --- ---	

Thou hast set me at the head of nations,		תשמני[100] לראש גים	3
A strange people serves me,		עם לא ידעתי יעבדני	3
As soon as they hear of me, they submit to me.	45	לשמע[101] אזן ישמעו לי	3
Foreigners fawn upon me,		בני[102] נכר יכחשו לי	3
Foreigners collapse before me,	46	בני נכר יבלו <לי>[103]	3
....		[104]____________[105]	
"By the life of Yahweh", blessed is my Rock,	47	חי יהוה[106] ⌈⌉ברך צרי	3
Exalted be the God of my salvation.		[107]ו⌈⌉ירם אלהי ישעי	3
He is the God who gives me vengeance	48	⌈⌉אל[108] ⌈⌉נתן נקמת לי	3
Who brings peoples down under me,		מרד[109] עמם תחתני	3
Who delivers me from my enemies	49a	{מצאי / מפלטי}[110] מאיבי	3
Over my adversaries Thou hast exalted me,	49b	מקמי[111] תרממני [][112]	3
Therefore I will praise thee among the nations,	50	על כן אדכה בגים	3
Yahweh, thy name will I celebrate in song,		יהוה[113] לשמכה אזמר	3
Who increases the victories of his king,	51	מגדל[114] ישעת מלכה[115]	3
Who shows favor to his anointed.		⌈⌉עשה חסד למשחה[116]	3

———

Notes to the Text

1. The poem has been reconstructed according to the orthography used in the Northern Kingdom (Israel) during the ninth-eighth centuries B.C. The general morphological and orthographic principles may be derived from the inscriptional material. A number of forms remain uncertain, however, because of the paucity of epigraphic evidence. Further discoveries of inscriptional data from this period may be expected to clarify the details; but the basic picture will be substantially unchanged. It is now quite certain that all final vowel sounds were indicated in the spelling: *i* by *yodh*, *u* by *waw*, the others, *a*, *e*, and *o* by *he*. *Matres lectionis* were not used to represent medial vowels in this period. We cannot determine the extent to which historical spellings were preserved or restored in the scribal practice of the day.

2. Verses 2-4 have been omitted from the text, because of the difficulty in reconstructing this poetic introduction in its original form. The general meaning of the passage is clear, but the precise relationship between the two texts (II Sam. and Psalm 18) can hardly be determined. A study of the parallel passages indicates that there were two early versions of the introduction (one apparently in the third person, the other in the second person). Neither of these is preserved intact in the present Massoretic texts. A third version of the same passage occurs in Psalm 144:2; it seems further removed from the original than the others, though retaining readings of value. We have in both II Sam. 22 and Psalm 18 a conflate text combining words and phrases from the older forms of the introduction. Any attempt at restoring the more original texts of the introduction must be labelled provisional. The following reconstruction is based upon the text of II Sam. 22, Psalms 18 and 144. The projected texts agree as to length and structure, represent a maximum variation as to content (insofar as these are attested by the existing texts--what other variations may have existed can only be surmised). Other possible reconstructions would fall somewhere within the limits represented by A. and B.

A

Yahweh is my Rock and Fastness,	יהוה סלעי ומצדתי	3
My Fort and my Deliverer is my God,	משגבי ומפלטי אלי	3
My Rock, in whom I trust	צרי אחסה-בה	2
My Savior, worthy of praise.	משעי מהלל	2
I call, O Yahweh,	אקרא יהוה	2
That from my enemies I may be saved.	מאיבי אושע	2

B

I will exalt thee, O Yahweh, my Strength	ארממכה יהוה חזקי	3
My Shield and my Horn of salvation,	מגני וקרן ישעי	3
My Fort and my Refuge,	משגבי ומנסי	2
My Savior, worthy of praise.	משעי מהלל	2
I call, O Yahweh,	אקרא יהוה	2
From violence thou dost save me.	מחמס תשעני	2

This reconstruction involves no emendations except for the commonly adopted ארממכה. There are, however, a series of rearrangements of different cola. The source of the readings can be ascertained at a glance by the reader (the second colon of *A* is taken from Ps. 144:2, *metri causa*; the others come from the texts in II Sam. 22 and Ps. 18); detailed explanations are unnecessary. The strophic arrangement, 3:3 followed by 2:2.2:2, though not duplicated precisely in this poem (cp., however, vss. 26-27), is common in ancient Hebrew poetry: Exod. 15, Jud. 5, and the Lament of David, II Sam. 1:19-27.

The reading ארממכה (*B*), was proposed by Hitzig, *Die Psalmen*, Leipzig and Heidelberg, 1863, *ad loc.*, and has since been accepted by most scholars; cf. Ps. 145:1. For the spelling of this word with final *he*, see footnote 66. On the spelling of בה (*A*), see footnote 34.

Of special interest for orthography are the words משעי and תשעני in II Sam. 22:3. These are spelled according to the practice of Israel in the ninth-eighth centuries, i.e. without orthographic indication of the contracted diphthong. In the South, diphthongs remained uncontracted. The words would have been pronounced *mawšīᶜî* and *tawšīᶜēnî*, and written מושעי and תושעני. Not until exilic or post-exilic times were these diphthongs contracted in Judah; then the *waw* was retained as a *mater lectionis* in the medial position, representing *ô*. Thus we get the normal Massoretic spelling: מֹושִׁעִי and תֹושִׁעֵנִי.

3. Omit the כי at the beginning of the verse, following Ps. 18; and the *waw* at the beginning of the second colon, following II Sam. 22. For discussion of the use of the conjunction at the beginning of cola, see the introductory notes; for the evidence of the versions, see the chart at the end of the study.

4. Read משברי with II Sam. 22; חבלי in Ps. 18 is secondary, apparently introduced from vs. 6.

The problem of the form of the ending of the construct plural of the masculine noun in Hebrew is perplexing. It is clear that in early Northwest Semitic, the ending was -*ū* for the nominative case, and -*ī* for the oblique cases. This pattern apparently holds for Ugaritic and South Canaanite (Amarna), though the vocalization of the oblique case ending is ambiguous. In Phoenician, the ending of the construct plural is not indicated in the orthography, thus showing that it was a vowel, presumably either *ī* or *ê*. In the Zinjirli inscriptions, Panammu I and II, the plural case endings of the masculine noun are certainly *ū* and *ī* (represented in the orthography by *waw* and *yodh*); cf. J. Friedrich, "Der Schwund kurzer Endvokale im Nordwestsemitischen", *ZS* I (1922), pp. 3-14 (he is nevertheless quite wrong in his major thesis). One may also compare the masculine plural construct endings in East and South Semitic. On the other hand, a secondary form of the construct plural appears in Aramaic, namely one ending in -*ay*. This is found in Syriac and in old "Reichsaramäisch", later contracted to -*ē* in West Aramaic dialects. Biblical Hebrew, according to the Massoretic vocalization, reads ֵי, presumably a contraction from -*ay* (cf. such forms as *sūsay*, *sūsayik*, etc.).

The matter, however, cannot be left there, because of a complicating factor in the Hebrew dialects. Inscriptional evidence for Judahite demonstrates that diphthongs remained uncontracted as late as the sixth century B.C. The masculine construct plural ending is represented by *yodh*, and is undoubtedly to be vocalized *-ay*; cf. Lachish Letter #6, line 5: ידיך, *yadayk*, and #6:12-13, אלהיך, *'elōhayk*. Later this was contracted to *-ê* producing Massoretic ֵי.

No inscriptional examples of the masculine construct plural have been found for the Northern dialect. It is clear, however, that the Bronze Age contraction of diphthongs, *ay* > *ê*, and *aw* > *ô*, took place in Israelite. If the form of the construct plural were originally the same as in Judahite, *ay*, then it would have become *-ê* in Israelite. The sound *ê* is everywhere in the inscriptional material, Aramaic, Moabite, Israelite, and Judahite, represented by the vowel letter *he*. This is so, regardless of the etymological origin of the sound. In the Hebrew Bible, moreover, *he* is the regular *mater lectionis* for final *-ê* in all cases, except those in which a late (exilic or after) secondary contraction, *ay* > *ê*, has taken place. In the latter, historical spelling preserves the original *yodh* representing the diphthong. In the light of this evidence, three possibilities exist with respect to the construct plural of masculine nouns in Israelite:

1) If the construct plural was pronounced *-ê* in Israelite, then in ninth-eighth century orthography it must have been indicated by *he*. The difficulty with this view is that no vestige of this orthography has survived in the Massoretic text. Rather the construct plural is consistently indicated by the vowel letter *yodh*.

2) If the construct plural ending in Israelite was indicated by *yodh*, then it must have been pronounced *ī*. This is the only vocalic value that *yodh* had in Northwest Semitic orthography during the ninth-sixth centuries. Morphologically such a form is tenable, and is in fact to be expected, as the data presented above show.

3) According to the orthodox position, the construct plural ending is held to have been pronounced *-ê*, and to have been indicated in the orthography by *yodh* (as in the Massoretic text). The defense for this explanation rests upon the basis of historical spelling: the *yodh* standing originally for the diphthong *-ay* was retained in the spelling after the diphthong was contracted to *-ê*. A parallel is drawn to a similar development in the contraction of medial diphthongs in post-exilic Judahite, e.g. בֵּית < *בַּיְת, the *yodh* being preserved as a *mater lectionis* for *ê*. The situation, however, is quite different. In the

latter case, the use of *matres lectionis*, final and medial, was already well established. At the time that the final diphthong *ay* contracted in Israelite, *matres lectionis* were not used at all, and the resulting vowel, *ê*, would not have been indicated by anything (as ample evidence from North and South Canaanite dialects, and the Israelite Gezer Calendar, show). Such an historical spelling (i.e., the retention or restoration of *yodh* as a vowel letter for final *ê* < *ay*) must bridge the gap between the period of diphthong contraction, before the fourteenth century B.C., and the introduction of final *matres lectionis* in the ninth century. Had the contraction of diphthongs taken place at the time of, or after, the introduction of *matres lectionis*, there might be some reason to expect instances of historical spelling; but not when a long period of strict phonetic consonantal orthography intervened. It is exceedingly difficult to suppose, therefore, that after five hundred years in which the final vowel was not represented at all, etymologic *yodh* was introduced to represent the construct plural ending, -*ê*, while in all other cases, final *ê* was represented by *he*.

It seems to the writers that the weight of evidence is in favor of the second possibility, namely that the construct plural ending of masculine nouns in Israelite was -*ī*, and that it was represented by *yodh* in the orthography of the ninth-eighth centuries. Such biblical formations as פנואל, *p^e nū'ēl* (in which the first element is certainly nominative construct plural, cp. Ugar. *pnm*, and Hebrew *pānîm*), and the more common form פניאל, *p^e nī'ēl* (the genitive plural construct form, preserved here, although the significance of the case ending was lost) are strong evidence for the existence of these construct plural forms in Hebrew.

Hence, vocalize **mišb^e rî*.

5. Vocalize *môt* (Ugar. *mt*); the diphthong was regularly contracted in Canaanite.

6. This passage supports the etymology of בליעל as proposed by the older scholars, i.e., **bal(i) ya^c l(ê)* = (place from which) none arises, a euphemism for Hades or Sheol. Hence, בני בליעל are simply "hellions".

7. Read the longer form סבבני (following Ps. 18), parallel with אפפני. Metrical requirements also enter into consideration.

8. Vocalize *môq^e šî* < **mawqišî*. Following the customary practice in Israel, there is no indication in the orthography of

the contracted diphthong, *aw* > *ô*, in the medial position. This spelling is preserved in II Sam. 22; Ps. 18 has the normal Judahite spelling. On the construct plural ending, see footnote 4.

9. אשוע in Ps. 18 is preferable. The LXX and Vulgate have different verbs in the two cola of vs. 7a, in the translation both of II Sam. 22 and Ps. 18, and thus support this reading.

10. The conjunction is to be omitted at the beginning of both cola, for metrical and stylistic reasons. For the evidence of the manuscripts and versions, see appended chart.

11. מהכלה refers to the heavenly abode of Yahweh, cf. Patton, *Canaanite Parallels in the Book of Psalms*, p. 21.

12. The diphthong *aw* is correctly preserved in שועתי (*aw* < *aww*); the *waw*, being consonantal, would naturally appear in the orthography.

13. לפנו תבא באזנו in Ps. 18 is a conflate text, combining the readings, תבא באזנו and לפנו תבא. One of these variants is indirectly supported by the text of II Sam. 22: שוע]תי בא[זנו; תבא has been completely lost by haplography. This haplography is more easily explained if we suppose that the *mater lectionis yodh* for final *î* did not appear in the master copy of the poem. This circumstance would suggest a tenth-century date for the manuscript, since final vowel letters were not indicated in the orthography in that period.

14. Omit the conjunction, *metri causa*; cf. the appended chart for the textual evidence.

15. Note the rhyme mechanism here; cp. also vss. 26-27, notes 59 and 60.

16. The article is extremely rare in ancient poetry, and does not belong here. In the course of transmission, there would naturally be a tendency to insert it.

17. Read הרם which fits the context better; cp. Deut. 32:22. The reading in II Sam. 22 (with the article) is suspicious. The Vulgate and the Peshitta (the text of II Sam. 22 in this version has been harmonized with that of Ps. 18) apparently read *hārîm* in both texts.

18. The repetition of the verb געש is suspicious.

19. These cola form a tricolon, the first of a number in this poem, vss. 12; 33, 34; 40, 41a; 41b, 43; 44c,d, 45a; 45b, 46; 48, 49a; 49b, 50. Note the sequence of verbal tenses (perfect, imperfect, perfect), without *waw* consecutive.

20. Vocalize *b^{e}'appêw, "from his nostrils" (reading the plural involves no change in the consonantal text). The preposition ב is used with the archaic meaning, "from", as also in vs. 14 and 16. This usage, together with other examples of archaic language and imagery in these lines, show strong affinities with old Canaanite poetry. In this instance, the preposition ב probably owes its preservation to the plausible misinterpretation of the phrase באפו, "in his anger" (cp., however, the parallel מפיהו). For the use of ב in Canaanite, see Albright, "The Phoenician Inscriptions of the Tenth Century B.C. from Byblus", p. 158, note 42. See also Chapter I, notes 64 and 65. The vocalization of the suffix follows the phonetic pattern of the dual in the North, with contraction of the diphthong (*-*ayhū* > *êhū* > **êw*), cf. Albright, "The Gezer Calendar", p. 22, note 27. In Judahite, where contraction did not take place, the form of the suffix seems to have been -*aw* < *-*ayhū*, with syncope of intervocalic *he* and *yodh* as in Aramaic.

21. It is perhaps preferable to read the older, fuller form of the suffix, for metrical reasons: *mippîhū*.

22. Omit initial *waw*; for the evidence, see the appended chart.

23. The meaning of this passage is explained by a similar passage in Isa. 63:19, לוא קרעת שמים ירדת מפנך הרים נזלו, "Verily thou hast torn open the heavens, thou hast come down; before thee the mountains shook". The sense of the verb יטה here must be, "to spread out, to spread apart, to spread open", as curtains. The same meaning occurs in the parallel passage, Ps. 144:5, יהוה הט שמיך ותרד גע בהרים ויעשנו, "O Yahweh, spread open thy heavens and come down; smite the mountains that they give forth smoke".

24. Read *yaṭṭê* or *yiṭṭê*

25. Omit the *waw* for stylistic reasons.

26. Omit the *waw* at the beginning of the colon. For biblical and Ugaritic parallels to this bicolon, cf. Patton, *Canaanite Parallels in the Book of Psalms*, p. 20.

27. Or perhaps read ^{c}*alê*, for metrical reasons, here and in the second colon. In the tenth century, both long and short forms would fall together in the orthography.

28. Read the plural, *k^{e}rūbîm*, following the versions.

29. יעף and ידאה are doublets (cf. vs. 17); וירא in II Sam. 22 is a scribal error (*resh* for *daleth*). On the other hand,

it is possible that the text is defective, and that the verbs יעף and ידאה originally governed separate but parallel cola. For literary parallels, see Patton, *op. cit.*, p. 36.

30. Omit the conjunction, following Ps. 18. See the appended chart.

31. סתרה in Ps. 18 is apparently an ancient variant of one or both of the following terms. It is curious that all three words begin with *samekh*, and some kind of dittography is also possible.

32. The word *sukkātô* is defectively written in II Sam. 22, i.e., the final vowel *ô* of the third person suffix is not indicated. It was only in the tenth century (and earlier) that final vowels were not indicated in the orthography. סכות in II Sam. 22 (the medial *waw* is a much later insertion) was reinterpreted, and thus the defective spelling was preserved.

33. *ḥašrat mêm* (contracted from *maym*) is the more difficult reading, and probably correct. *ḥeškat* in Ps. 18 has apparently been substituted under the influence of *ḥōšek* earlier in the verse. The word has falsely been connected with Accadian *ašâru*, Arabic *ḥašara*. It is etymologically related to Neo-Hebrew חשרה, "sieve", and חשר, which is used occasionally of clouds sifting or distilling water (cp. the Vulgate translation, *cribrans*). Ugaritic *ḫṯr* also fits into the picture, with the meaning "sieve" or the like. In the present context, the phrase must refer to the clouds as the sieve-like containers from which the rainwater drops.

34. *^{c}abî š^{e}ḥāqîm* is extra-metrical in vs. 12, and belongs rather with the following words. Ps. 18 has a conflate text, with two variants of this colon: עבי שחקים מנגה and נגדו עביו עברו. מנגה is a corruption of *negdô*, the initial *mem* being due to dittography of the final *mem* of the preceding word; the final *he* is correct for the third person singular suffix in pre-exilic times. Cp. Cheyne's remarks on this verse in *The Book of Psalms*, London, 1892, I, *ad loc.* The text of II Sam. 22 has suffered serious haplography, due to the sequence of words with the same letters. The resultant text in II Sam. 22 בערו גחלי-אש has undoubtedly been influenced by the reading גחלים בערו in vs. 9.

35. Read בשמם with Ps. 18. ב is used here with the archaic meaning, "from", as in Ugaritic. In the text of II Sam. 22, we have an instance of editorial revision (substitution of

min). Cf. Patton, *op. cit.*, p. 18, for the meaning of the phrase.

36. ברד וגחלי-אש is a dittography from vs. 13. The whole of vs. 14 has a strong Canaanite flavor (adapted to the Yahwistic religion); cp. Ugaritic 51:V:70,71; 51:VII:28-31; also Ps. 29:3. The whole of Psalm 29, as pointed out by Ginsberg (*Kitvê Ugarit*, Jerusalem, 1936, pp. 129ff.) is an adaptation of an old Canaanite poem. On this point, see also T. H. Gaster's "Psalm 29", *JQR* 37 NS (1946), pp. 55-65; and Patton, *op. cit.*, pp. 25f., 30, 34, 38.

37. Omit the conjunction at the beginning of both cola. For the evidence, see the appended chart.

38. חציו and חצים are apparently old variants; there must also have been parallel variants ברקם and ורקו in the second colon; but cp. Ps. 144:6. For literary parallels, cf. Patton, *op. cit.*, pp. 22f.

39. ברק has evidently been lost by haplography in Ps. 18, רב being simply a remnant of the older reading. In II Sam. 22, on the other hand, ברקם (or ברקו), seems to have been lost, also by haplography (so Nowack and others). Cp. the use of the verb with the cognate accusative in Ps. 144:6.

40. Omit the conjunction, for metrical reasons.

41. Read *'ᵃpîqî-m yām*, "the sources (springs) of the sea". The enclitic *mem* was preserved in the text of Ps. 18, although not understood as such; the result was the misinterpretation *mayim*. The text of II Sam. 22 was revised in accordance with a correct understanding of the meaning of the passage; the superfluous *mem* was omitted. On the use of the enclitic *mem* in a construct chain, cf. Albright, "Oracles of Balaam", p. 219, note 83, "The Old Testament and the Canaanite Language", pp. 23f., and Patton, *op. cit.*, p. 12, where this occurrence is cited. Literary parallels to this couplet abound in Ugaritic literature (cf. Patton, *op. cit.*, pp. 29, 34). Cp. II Dan. VI:48 = 'nt V:15, where *'apq thmtm* and *gly* occur in close association; *msdt 'arṣ* also occurs in Ugaritic.

42. The preposition ב meaning "from" has been preserved in the text of II Sam. 22, cf. footnote 35. There were two variant forms of this bicolon, one in the second person (Ps. 18), the other in the third person (II Sam. 22). In the third person variant, the first colon is too short. Perhaps פני has dropped

out after בגערת; cp. Ps. 80:17. For the spelling of the second person singular suffix -כה, cf. footnote 66.

43. Read the dual, "thy nostrils", as in Exod. 15:8. The omission of the *yodh* (for the contracted diphthong of the dual, *ay* > *ê*) is typical of Israelite orthography, as against Judahite where the *yodh* regularly appears in pre-exilic inscriptions (indicating the uncontracted diphthong *ay*, as in ידיך in the Lachish Letters).

44. Insert ידה, *yādô*, "his hand", following the parallel passage in Ps. 144:7 (so Nowack and others). This is the standard idiom.

45. מרם, corresponding to Ugar. *mrym*, is a common term for the region of the divine abode. Cf. Patton, *op. cit.*, pp. 19, 20.

46. יקחני and ימשני are evidently old variants; other readings are to be found in Ps. 144:7. ימשני is probably the original reading, as the *lectio difficilior*.

47. Read the plural, following the versions, and as implied in the parallel colon.

48. This reconstruction is based upon the parallel in the second colon: the words כי עזו actually occur in the Targum (according to the apparatus in BH^3 for Ps. 18). The כי has dropped out as a result of homoioteleuton. עז is defective spelling for *ᶜazzû*, an indication of a tenth-century date for the writing down of this poem.

49. As the context shows, these verbs are to be understood as having a past meaning. See the Introduction, notes *y* and *z*.

50. משען לי (II Sam. 22) is one variant reading, perhaps original. The text of Ps. 18 is a conflate, combining the reading in II Sam. 22, and one in which the order of the words was reversed, לְ משען, in the defective orthography of the tenth century.

51. Omit the *waw* for stylistic reasons. The reading in Ps. 18 (with the verbal suffix) is preferable to that in II Sam. 22 (with the sign of the accusative and the independent pronoun). The colon in Ps. 18, however, is short, and a third word may have dropped out. A suggestion is *merḥăbê 'ereṣ*, as in Habakkuk 1:6. This may also explain the corruption in the text of II Sam. 22 (subsequently revised). ויצא in Ps. 18 is an instance of Israelite orthography of the ninth-eighth centuries.

52. Read כצדקי following Ps. 18, *metri causa*. In the matter of a single syllable, however, there can be no certainty.

53. The use of the preposition *min* following the verb *rš*[c] is strange, and otherwise unattested in the Old Testament. Read probably, therefore, פשעתי, as suggested by Prof. Albright, who compares the usage of פשע with מן in II Kings 8:20, 22.

54. The *kethib* in II Sam. 22 preserves the pre-exilic spelling of the suffix without the *mater lectionis yodh*. Vocalize *mišpāṭîw* (< *mišpāṭī-hū*; cf. footnote 4). This form is parallel to Judahite *mišpāṭâw* (< *mišpāṭay-hū*).

55. A *mem* seems to have dropped out by haplography in Ps. 18. II Sam. 22 apparently has preserved a conflate text, reading *mimmênî* as in Ps. 18 (after *'asīr*), and אָסוּר מֵ[ה]ֵנָּה, utilizing the longer form of the third person feminine plural suffix, which undoubtedly occurred more often in Hebrew poetry than is commonly supposed; other examples occur in Isa. 34:16, Jer. 5:6, etc. The newly discovered Isaiah scroll swarms with such spellings. A parallel to the reading in Ps. 18 is found in Job 27:5.

56. Omit the conjunction here and at the beginning of the second colon also, for stylistic reasons.

57. Read the longer form אהיה with II Sam. 22, for metrical reasons. There seems to be no reason for the cohortative אשתמרה. It may be pointed out that these long and short forms would fall together in tenth-century orthography.

58. We would hardly expect the pronominal suffix here. It is perhaps more likely that an old genitive case ending has been preserved.

59. Verse 25 seems out of place in the present context. Moreover, its verbal connections with vs. 21 suggest that it is a doublet.

60. Omit גב(ו)ר which breaks into the rhythm and disturbs the balance of the phrases (this omission is supported by the Peshitta for Ps. 18). As pointed out in the introduction, these couplets (vs. 26-27) are apparently an old gnomic quatrain, quoted in the psalm. We would expect the metrical form of such couplets to be quite rigid, and marked by assonance and alliteration, if not rhyme.

61. The strange verbal forms preserved in II Sam. 22 (תתבר and תתפל) can hardly be the result of textual corruption, although the standard forms appear in Ps. 18. The rhythmic pattern

of the forms in II Sam. 22 (agreeing with *tittammām*) suggests that we have in this text a transcription of the spoken couplet; while in Ps. 18 we have the correct grammatical or literary form (so substantially Delitzsch). Zorell's interpretation of vs. 27, *Biblica* 9 (1928), p. 224, does not commend itself.

62. The כי of Ps. 18 is apparently due to dittography (cp. vs. 29, 30); the conjunction in II Sam. 22 is likewise to be omitted, see the appended chart. Read *'attâ* with Ps. 18; את in II Sam. 22 is not the sign of the accusative, but rather the pronoun written defectively (so Briggs).

63. The text of Ps. 18 is grammatically sound, though employing highly poetic language: "and the haughty eyes thou humblest". The text of II Sam. 22 is corrupt, and involves at least one additional variant reading. By combining the texts of II Sam. 22 and Ps. 18, we get *ᶜênê-m rāmîm tašpîl*, "the haughty-eyed thou humblest" (with enclitic *mem* in the construct chain). The reading suggested by O. H. Böstrom, *Alternative Readings in the Hebrew of the Books of Samuel*, Rock Island, 1918, p. 57, (עניך על-רמים, "thine eyes are upon the haughty") is not satisfactory. Klostermann's emendation seems better: עני כ[]ל-רמים (cited from Nowack, *Richter, Ruth u. Bücher Samuelis*, p. 247). This may represent a third variant reading.

64. The present text of Ps. 18 is unintelligible; it can be most easily explained as a corrupt conflate of variant readings, one of which is preserved in the text of II Sam. 22. The other variant read originally כ-את אר יהו (following tenth-century orthography); the *taw* of תא[י]ר is an instance of dittography after את. The word אֹרִ, "my light", is a variant of נֵרִ. The absence of the *mater lectionis yodh* (for the pronominal suffix) is also explicable on the basis of tenth-century orthography.

65. אלהי is the preferable reading here.

66. This verse has never been satisfactorily explained. One frequently proposed emendation (most recently Schmidt and Buttenwieser) is ארץ גדר, "I break through a wall" (indirectly supported by the reading in the Lucianic text, πεφραγμένος, "fenced, fortified", for II Sam. 22). Fleet's interpretation of the first colon (*Expository Times*, XLII [1930-31], p. 526), does not help materially. The verse must be interpreted as a unit, and fitted into the context.

The spelling of the word בכה (II Sam. 22) is noteworthy. The more elegant literary form of the suffix was *-kā*, and this is the proper spelling of that form after the tenth century. The shortened form, *-ak*, already current in pre-exilic times (in popular speech), was spelled כ as attested in the Lachish Letters. An examination of the new Maccabaean manuscripts, especially the Isaiah scrolls, indicates that there were two orthographic traditions: one which preferred *plene* writing in general, and emphasized the longer final forms such as כה, to the extent of displacing the shorter forms even where the latter were original; the other had the opposite tendency, making the shorter final forms, like כ, standard. The *textus receptus* of the Massoretes follows, in the main, the second tradition, with numerous exceptions, however. The Massoretic pointing, ךָ, on the other hand, is in line with the first tradition. The Massoretes simply restored the older literary pronunciation, *-kā*, most probably on the basis of old manuscripts (like the first Isaiah scroll) in which the suffix was spelled out in full. They had no authority, however, to revise the orthography (i.e., to change the consonants and vowel letters) of the *textus receptus*, and were content to indicate the proper vocalization by use of the anomalous *qameṣ* in the bosom of the *kaph*. It is to be noted that the earlier Palestinian punctuators made the vocalization of the suffix conform to the received spelling (i.e., *-ak*, cf. Kahle, *The Cairo Geniza*, pp. 97ff., and references there). A similar line of reasoning would apply to the other anomalous pointings in the Massoretic text: the perfect form of the verb, second masculine singular, and the third person feminine singular pronominal suffix with plural nouns.

67. Vs. 31a is strikingly parallel to Deut. 32:4 and it is quite possible, therefore, that a second colon has fallen out in this poem. At the same time, vs. 31b and c are almost exactly the same as Prov. 30:5 (the meter of which is superior). The textual history of this verse is very complex; in its present form in II Sam. 22 = Psalm 18, it is not above suspicion.

68. Following Prov. 30:5.

69. Omit כי for stylistic reasons; so also the LXX and Vulgate (II Sam. 22).

70. Omit the *waw* for stylistic reasons.

71. Following the text of Ps. 18.

72. This verse is emended on the basis of the closely parallel phrase in the old hymn found in Hab. 3. יהוה in Hab. 3:19 is perhaps preferable to האל which may have crept in under the influence of האל in vs. 31. This also seems to be true of the last two words of vs. 33, which are reminiscent of תמים דרכו in vs. 31; see footnote 75.

73. מעזי is preferable to the reading in Ps. 18, המאזרני, which seems to have arisen under the influence of תאזרני in vs. 40. In this context, the use of the article is suspicious.

74. The reading וחלי follows, in part, the text of Hab. 3:19. The absence of the *mater lectionis yodh* to indicate the suffix may be explained as an instance of tenth-century orthography.

75. A tricolon is expected on the basis of the Habakkuk passage. The verbs ויתן and ויתר ("to cause to spring up") are probably variants of מאוה, and וישם (Hab. 3:19). The phrase תמם דרכו is clearly out of place; cp. vs. 31.

76. The suffix of the first person is to be read following Ps. 18 and Habakkuk 3. II Sam. 22 apparently preserves a third person variant (referring to the king?).

77. The suffix is difficult to construe. The *yodh* may have been inserted on the basis of Hab. 3 where it marks the construct plural before a word which has since dropped out. Cf. footnote 78.

78. On the evidence of Job 9:8, Prof. Albright has reconstructed the last colon of Hab. 3:19 to read על במתי <ים>, "on the back of Sea". This phrase has a mythological background referring to the struggle of the great god with the sea-dragon; here, however, it refers to the more general human conquest of the terrors of sea travel, etc., and finally becomes a poetic phrase for "victory". The present text may be explained on this basis. It is also possible, however, that the word <מת> has dropped out by simple haplography. The metaphor is perhaps less strained if we read "Death", since the victory of the individual rather than the victory of Yahweh is involved. It may be observed that the struggle between Baal and Yam is paralleled in Ugaritic by the struggle between Baal and Mot. Cassuto and Albright have also noted the occurrence of מת as "Death personified" (i.e., as a sea-dragon) in Hab. 3:13. Albright renders:

Thou didst smite the head of wicked Death,	מחצת ראש מות-רשע
Destroying him tail-end to neck!	ערת יסוד עד צואר

It is also personified in vs. 6 of this poem. The spelling מת is, of course, correct for Israelite as also Ugaritic and Phoenician.

For the figure of a man trampling on the back of his foe, cf. Deut. 33:29.

79. As it stands, vs. 35 does not make suitable sense. Previous commentators have emended the text drastically, without, however, producing satisfactory results. The clue to the correct reconstruction is to be found in Ps. 144:1, a parallel verse: המלמד ידי לקרב אצבעותי למלחמה. לקרב אצבעותי has dropped out of our poem by haplography (note the sequence *yodh lamedh*). The phrase ונחת(ה) קשת נחושה is misplaced and belongs properly after vs. 36a. The final word זרעתי belongs with למלחמה; the two words constitute a variant reading parallel with המלמד ידי לקרב. In either case, the second colon is a ballast variant of the first, the two longer words more than balancing the three short ones of the first colon.

80. Omit the conjunction; for the evidence of the versions, see the appended chart. Vs. 35b, which does not yield sense in its present position (cf. footnote 79), fits very nicely after vs. 36a, as a ballast variant. With this verse begins the preparation of the warrior for battle, by his Lord. This theme is common to ancient mythology, Canaanite, Greek, etc. Cf. L. Dürr, "Zum altorientalischen Gedankkreis: 'Der König als Meister im Bogenschiessen von der Gottheit unterrichtet'", *OLZ*, XXXIV (1931), col. 697. The description of the arming of the warrior in vss. 36-37 is followed by a vivid picture of the hero in action, vss. 38-39. The remainder of the poem reviews the rewards bestowed upon the victor, the sorry state of the conquered; it closes with praise to Yahweh for granting victory.

81. By transposing the first two consonants of the word ונחת (II Sam. 22), we get *ḥ*^{a}*nît*, "javelin", one in the series of weapons and armor with which the warrior is equipped. The resulting phrase, "javelin and bow of bronze", makes excellent sense after 36a; cf. Ps. 46:10, Jud. 5:8 for general parallels. The expression, "bow of bronze", is, of course, hyperbolical, cf. Job 20:24.

82. This colon has accidentally dropped out of II Sam. 22.

83. The word is difficult. Prof. Albright derives it from the root ^{c}*ny*; it is related to $^{c}\bar{e}t$ (for *^{c}*int*), "time", Assyrian *ettu*, "sign, omen"; also Canaanite ^{c}*Anat*, which originally meant "sign, indication of purpose, providence". For discussion of this point, see his *Archaeology and the Religion of Israel*, p. 195, note 14. "Providence" or "will" fits the context very well here. The vocalization is uncertain, but there is no reason to suppose that the *waw* in Ps. 18 is original.

84. *taḥtēnî* appears in the text of II Sam. 22 here and in vs. 40 and 48, but nowhere else in the Old Testament. The normal form appears in Ps. 18, *taḥtay*. There is reason to believe that the form in II Sam. 22 is dialectal (i.e., Israelite). This view is supported by the appearance of the same form, תחתנ, *taḥtēnī*, in the Kilamuwa Inscription, line 14, a Canaanite stele from the ninth century.

85. It is difficult to choose between the long and short forms; perhaps *'erdōp* is preferable here. The passage is closely paralleled in Exod. 15:9, where we have a staccato style (2:2), without any conjunctions.

86. אשמדם and אשגם are old variants.

87. Read, perhaps, the longer, poetic form ^{c}*adê*, *metri causa*.

88. The association of כלה and מחץ is common in Ugaritic. II Sam. 22 clearly preserves a conflate text. ואכלם appears to be secondary, inserted under the influence of כלותם in the preceding verse. For literary parallels, see Patton, *Canaanite Parallels in the Book of Psalms*, p. 40.

89. Either variant is possible. Perhaps יקמן is preferable for metrical reasons.

90. Read the contracted (spoken) form, תזרני, preserved in II Sam. 22. Ps. 18 retains the correct grammatical form, i.e., *piel* imperfect. On the presence of the popular, spoken forms in the text of II Sam. 22, see footnote 61. The meter requires the short form: *tazrēnî* < **ta'azzirēnî*.

91. The form *nātattā* is spelled in two different ways in the Massoretic text, נתתה and נתת. The spelling נתתה is correct post-tenth century orthography for the longer vocalization, *nātattā*. The spelling נתת presupposes the shorter vocalization, *nātat*. Throughout the received text, the short form (in the

orthography, not the vocalization) has generally displaced the longer literary form, with final *he*. For certain verbs, however, among them *nātan*, the longer form has been preserved in a majority of the cases. The precise reason for this cannot now be ascertained, but it may reflect the actual survival of the longer form in speech after the loss of the ending in other verbs. תתה in II Sam. 22 seems to be an error; conceivably we should read יתתה (initial *yodh* being lost by haplography), a Canaanite dialectal form (root, *ytn*), as in Ugaritic and Phoenician.

92. The rearrangement of the cola is dictated by sense and stylistic considerations. Vs. 42 is clearly out of place between vss. 41 and 43 (both in the first person), while vs. 41b forms an excellent tricolon with vs. 43a and b.

93. It is to be observed that although the first colon contains only two words, the syllable count of all three cola is identical (7:7:7). Symmetry in length in parallel cola is an exceedingly important criterion for the analysis of Old Canaanite and Hebrew poetry. Study of Ugaritic poetry has shown that three stresses may be distributed between two words. For literary parallels, especially in connection with the allegedly "late" word, צמת, see Patton, *Canaanite Parallels in the Book of Psalms*, p. 44.

94. There seems no reason to abandon the reading in II Sam. 22, which is metrically most suitable. The popular emendation of the text of Ps. 18: כעפר רחב is possible as a variant of כעפר ארץ. The present reading in Ps. 18 is a corruption of the similar phrase in vs. 11.

95. In the two texts, there are three variant readings, all apparently derived from the same original. From the textual point of view, any one of the three may be regarded as the original reading, and the others explained as corruptions of it. From the context, and the parallel verb in vs. 43a, אדקם would seem to be the preferred reading. ארקם would then arise as the result of the confusion between *resh* and *daleth*, common in all periods of Hebrew writing; ארקעם would enter the picture as a correction of the admittedly wrong ארקם.

96. משע is another case of early (ninth-eighth century) Israelite orthography. The diphthong *aw* has been contracted to *ô*, and this is not indicated in the spelling.

97. Following the text of II Sam. 22. Ps. 18 may have read simply ל, the *ayin* being a case of dittography.

98. The text presents a number of problems. Something seems to have dropped out after the first colon. תשמרני, which does not fit with the following words may be the first word of the missing colon, the other words having dropped out by haplography, between תשמרני and תשמני. The missing material may be in vs. 49, as has been suggested by a number of scholars. Vs. 49c fits very well after vs. 44a, but is out of place where it stands. We would then have the following variant readings: מאש חמסם תצלני and תשמרני מאש חמסם. For a parallel to this passage, see Ps. 140:5.

99. The defective spelling עם in Ps. 18 may be an instance of tenth-century orthography. The final *î*, which seems to be the case ending here rather than the pronominal suffix, would not have been indicated in the spelling of that period.

100. Following the order of the cola in Ps. 18:44b-46, we find a pair of tricola. The second of these preserves a characteristic pattern of ancient Hebrew and Canaanite poetry; cf. footnote 102.

101. Vocalize *lišmō*^{c}, following the text of II Sam. 22; the defective writing may be responsible for the different pointing in Ps. 18.

102. This tricolon follows the pattern, abc:abd:EF (ballast variant). This type of poetic structure is standard in Ugaritic and old Hebrew poetry. For a detailed discussion of these patterns, especially in old Hebrew poetry, see Prof. Albright's forthcoming article, "The Psalm of Habakkuk".

103. It is not necessary to change the verbal form, since the root *nbl* stands as an excellent parallel to *kḥš*. The second colon seems too short, however, and we ought perhaps to supply לי, the loss of which may be explained by haplography (in tenth-century orthography the final vowel letters would not have appeared, and the text would have read יִבְּלוּ לִי. Cf. Albright, "Are the Ephod and the Teraphim Mentioned in the Ugaritic Literature?", *BASOR* #83 (1941), p. 40, note 7.

Also possible is Nestle's emendation (*ZAW* 16 [1896], p. 324), יֹבִלוּ <שַׁי>. If the vocalization, *yôbīlû*, is correct, then the spelling יבלו is an example of ninth-eighth century Israelite orthography. For parallels to the phrase in question, see Ps. 68:30 and 76:12.

104. The interpretation of this colon is difficult. The parallel in Micah 7:17 tends to confirm the text, but does not in itself clear up the problems. The verb in Ps. 18, יחרגו is to be interpreted in the light of ירגזו (Mic. 7:17). יחגרו in II Sam. 22 apparently means "to stumble, limp" (i.e., to be bound of foot).

105. The precise significance of the word is not known. The suffix is written defectively in II Sam. 22, and is to be read, probably, *$\hat{i}m\bar{o}$ < *$\hat{i}$-*him*(*m*)*u* = Judahite **ay-him*(*m*)*u*, later Hebrew -*ēmô* (the poetic form). Ps. 18, on the other hand, has the normal prose form, יהם-. Cp. במתימו in the Massoretic text of Deut. 33:29 with במתם which appears in the Samaritan.

106. Omit the conjunction, which has no place in the text.

107. Omit the conjunction (see the appended chart), and read the jussive, *yārōm*.

108. The article is not expected in early poetry. The meter also is improved by the omission of them here.

109. *môrīd* appears without the *waw* in the Ben Chayyim edition of the Hebrew text of II Sam. 22. This shows that some manuscripts preserved the defective spelling, although the Ben Asher text which forms the basis for BH^3 spells the word מוריד. The defective spelling points to an early Israelite recension of the poem. Ps. 18 reads וידבר following the parallel passage in Ps. 47:4. Here, however, the participle is required. For another excellent variant, cf. Ps. 144:2. The root *yrd* is used in a similar sense in Ps. 56:8, Isa. 63:6, etc.

110. The variant readings are equally acceptable.

111. The shorter reading of II Sam. 22, מקמי (omitting the *waw*), is preferable, *metri causa*.

112. The third colon is out of place. It is hardly climactic after vs. 49a and b; cf. footnote 98. The words חמסם and חמס are apparently genuine variants. It is barely possible that the longer form is to be read *ḥāmās-m*(*i*), i.e., the singular (as in Ps. 18), with the enclitic particle. However, the relatively frequent occurrence of the plural form in similar constructions (e.g., Ps. 140:5) tends to rule out this possibility.

113. Omit the conjunction for the sake of parallelism.

114. Read *magdīl* following Ps. 18 and the *kethib* of II Sam. 22.

115. The word may be read *malkô* or *molkô*, and the phrase translated, "the victories of his king", or "the victories of his kingdom".

116. The word *mešîḥô* is not at all out of place in an early psalm. The term occurs regularly in the "court history" of King David (II Sam. 9-20, I Kings 1-2). The final colon of the poem, however, is suspicious, and may not belong to the original text.

TABLE

THE EVIDENCE FOR THE USE OF THE CONJUNCTION AT THE BEGINNING OF COLA

TABLE

The Evidence for the Use of the Conjunction at the Beginning of Cola, in the Hebrew Text and the Principal Versions

In the following table, the evidence is given for the use of the conjunction at the beginning of each colon from vs. 4 to the end of the poem. If no conjunction appears, that fact is indicated by a dash (-); if the conjunction does appear, it is indicated by the following signs: *w* for MT (Hebrew), *kai* for LXX (Greek), *et* for V (Latin), and *w* for S (Syriac); other particles are transliterated. Variant readings are indicated in parentheses beneath the standard text.

For MT, BH^3 was used. Variant readings were derived from the critical apparatus of BH^3, and of C. D. Ginsburg's *The Old Testament diligently revised according to the Masorah, etc.*, London, 1926. Additional readings were found in G. B. de Rossi's *Variae Lectiones Veteris Testamenti*, Parma, 1785.

For the LXX, the text of Codex Vaticanus (*B*) was followed. Variant readings for the text of II Samuel 22 were taken from the critical apparatus of the Cambridge Edition of the Septuagint, *The Old Testament in Greek*, ed. by A. E. Brooke, N. McLean and H. St. John Thackeray, Vol. II, Part I (I and II Samuel), Cambridge, 1927; and for Psalm 18, from the apparatus in Swete's edition of the *Old Testament in Greek*, Vol. II (3rd ed.), Cambridge, 1907, and Rahlfs' *Septuaginta*, Vol. II, Stuttgart, 1935.

For the Latin, the standard Clementine edition of the Vulgate has been used in the case of II Samuel 22. Variant readings were derived from C. Vercellone's *Variae Lectiones Vulgatae Latinae Bibliorum*, Vol. II, Rome, 1864. In the case of Psalm 18, P. de Lagarde's critical edition of the *Psalterium iuxta Hebraeos Hieronymi* was used. Variant readings were derived from the critical apparatus, Vercellone's material, and the Latin column of E. Nestle's *Psalterium Tetraglottum*, Tübingen, 1879.

For the Peshitta, the facsimile edition of the Codex Ambrosianus, published by Ceriani in two vols., 1876-1883, was used. Variant readings were taken from the standard edition of the Peshitta published by S. Lee in London, 1823, and from the critical apparatus in W. E. Barnes, *The Peshitta Psalter*, Cambridge, 1904.

The significant statistical data are given in the introduction. The numerical figures at the end of the chart indicate, 1) the total number of cola (106 in II Samuel 22, 107 in Psalm 18, not including vs. 14c which clearly is a case of dittography), 2) the number of times the conjunction appears at the beginning of cola (the figure under each column) and 3) the total number of conjunctions including variant readings (the figure in parentheses). For statistical purposes, particles other than the ordinary conjunction, "and", are largely disregarded.

Verse: Colon	II Samuel 22 MT	LXX	V	S	Psalm 18 MT	LXX	V	S
4:1	-	-	-	-	-	-	-	-
4:2	w	kai	et	w	w	kai	et	w
5:1	kî	oti (-)	quia	mĕṭul	- (kî)	-	-	mĕṭul
5:2	-	- (kai)	- (et)	w	w	kai	et	w
6:1	-	-	-	-	-	-	-	w (-)
6:2	-	- (kai)	-	w	-	-	-	w
7:1	-	-	- (et)	-	-	kai (-)	- (et)	-
7:2	w	kai	et	w	w	kai	et	w
7:3	w	kai (-)	et	w	-	- (kai)	-	w
7:4	w	kai	et	w	w	kai	et	w
8:1	w	kai	-	- (w)	w	kai (-)	-	-
8:2	- (w)	kai	- (et)	w	w	kai	et	w
8:3	w	kai	et	w	w	kai (-)	et	w
9:1	-	-	-	-	-	-	-	-
9:2	w	kai	et	w	w	kai	et	w
9:3	-	-	-	w	-	-	-	w
10:1	w	kai	- (et)	w	w	kai	-	-
10:2	w	kai	et (-)	w	w	kai	et	w

	II Samuel 22				*Psalm 18*			
V:C	*MT*	*LXX*	*V*	*S*	*MT*	*LXX*	*V*	*S*
11:1	w	kai	et	- (w)	w	kai	et	-
11:2	w	kai	et	w	w	- (kai)	et (-)	w
12:1	w	kai	- (et)	w	- (w)	kai	-	-
12:2	-	- (kai)	-	-	-	-	-	w (-)
13:1	-	-	-	-	-	-	-	-
13:2	-	-	-	-	-	-	-	-
14:1	-	- (kai)	-	w	w	kai	et	w
14:2	w	kai	et	w	w	kai	et	w
15:1	w	kai (-)	-	-	w	kai (-)	et	-
15:2	-	- (kai)	-	w (-)	w	kai	- (et)	-
16:1	w	kai	et	w	w	kai	et	w
16:2	-	kai	et	w	w	kai	et	w
16:3	-	-	-	-	-	-	-	-
16:4	-	- (kai)	- (et)	w	-	-	-	w
17:1	-	- (kai)	-	-	-	-	-	-
17:2	-	- (kai)	et (-)	w	-	-	- (et)	w
18:1	-	-	-	w	-	-	-	w
18:2	- (w)	- (kai)	et	w	w (-)	kai	et	w

	II Samuel 22				*Psalm 18*			
V:C	*MT*	*LXX*	*V*	*S*	*MT*	*LXX*	*V*	*S*
19:1	-	-	-	w	-	-	-	-
19:2	w	kai	et	w	w	kai	et	w
20:1	w	kai	et	w	w	kai	et	w
20:2	-	kai (-)	-	w	-	-	-	w
21:1	-	kai	-	w	-	kai	-	w
21:2	-	- (kai)	et	w	-	kai	- (et)	w
22:1	kî	oti	quia	mĕṭul	kî	oti	quia	mĕṭul
22:2	w	kai	et	w	w	kai	et	w
23:1	kî	oti	enim	mĕṭul	kî	oti	enim	mĕṭul
23:2	w	kai	et	w	w	kai	et	w
24:1	w	kai	et	w	w	kai	et	w
24:2	w	kai	et	w	w	kai	et	w
25:1	w	kai	et	w	w	kai	- (et)	w
25:2	-	kai	et	w	-	kai	- (et)	w
26:1	-	-	-	-	-	- (kai)	-	-
26:2	- (w)	kai	et	w	- (w)	kai	- (et)	w
27:1	-	kai	- (et)	w (-)	-	kai	- (et)	w
27:2	w	kai	et	w	w	kai	et	w
28:1	w	kai (oti)	et	mĕṭul	kî	oti	quia	mĕṭul

	II Samuel 22				Psalm 18			
V:C	MT	LXX	V	S	MT	LXX	V	S
28:2	w	kai	-que	w	w	kai	et	w
29:1	kî	oti	quia	-	kî	oti	quia	-
29:2	w	kai (-)	et (-)	-	-	-	-	w (-)
30:1	kî	oti	enim (-)	mĕṭul	kî	oti	enim	mĕṭul
30:2	- (w)	kai	-	w	w	kai	et	w
31:1	-	-	-	-	-	-	-	-
31:2	-	-	-	-	-	-	-	-
31:3	-	-	-	w	-	-	-	w
32:1	kî	- (oti)	- (quoniam)	mĕṭul	kî	oti	- (quoniam)	mĕṭul
32:2	w	kai	et	w	w	kai	et	w
33:1	-	-	-	-	-	-	-	-
33:2	w	kai	et	w	w	kai	et	w
34:1	-	-	-	w (-)	-	-	-	-
34:2	w	kai	et	w	w	kai	et	w
35:1	-	-	-	w (-)	-	-	-	-
35:2	w	kai	et	w	w	kai	et	w
36:1	w	kai	- (et)	w	w	kai	-	-
36:2				- (w)	w	kai	et	-
36:3	w	kai	et	w	w	kai	et	w

V:C	*II Samuel 22*				*Psalm 18*				
	MT	*LXX*	*V*	*S*	*MT*	*LXX*	*V*	*S*	
37:1	-	- (kai)	-	-	-	-	-	-	
37:2	w	kai	et	d	w	kai	et	d	
38:1	-	-	-	-	-	- (kai)	-	-	
38:2	w	kai (-)	et	w	w	kai	et	w	
39:1	w	kai	-	-	-	-	-	-	
39:2	w (-)	kai	-	w	-	-	-	w	
40:1	w	kai (-)	- (et)	-	w	kai	- (et)	-	
40:2	-	- (kai)	-	w	-	-	-	w	
41:1	w	kai	-	w	w	kai	-	w	
41:2	-	- (kai)	- (et)	w	w (-)	kai	et	w	
42:1	-	-	-	-	-	-	-	-	
42:2	-	-	-	w	-	-	-	-	
43:1	w	kai (-)	-	-	w	kai	-	-	
43:2	-	-	-	w	-	-	-	w	
44:1	w	kai (-)	-	-	-	-	-	-	
44:2	-	- (kai)	-	w (-)	-	-	-	w	
44:3	-	-	-	-	-	-	-	-	
45:1	-	-	-	[-	-	-	-	-]	45:2
45:2	-	-	-	[w (-)	-	-	-	w]	45:1

	II Samuel 22				*Psalm 18*				
V:C	*MT*	*LXX*	*V*	*S*	*MT*	*LXX*	*V*	*S*	
46:1	-	-	-	-	-	-	-	-	
46:2	w	kai (-)	et	w	w	kai	et	w	
47:1	-	-	-	-	-	-	-	-	
47:2	w	kai	et	w (-)	w	kai	et	-	
48:1	-	-	-	-	-	-	-	-	
48:2	w	- (kai)	et	w (-)	w	kai	et	w	
49:1	w	kai	-	w (-)	-	-	-	w	
49:2	w	kai	et	w	ʼap	- (kai)	et	w	
49:3	- (w)	-	-	w	-	-	-	w	
50:1	-	-	-	mĕṭul	-	-	-	mĕṭul	
50:2	w	kai	et	w	w	kai	et	w	
51:1	-	-	-	-	-	-	-	-	
51:2	w	kai	et	w	w	kai	et	w	
51:3	-	-	-	-	-	-	-	-	
106	47 (52)	54 (69)	41 (51)	66 (69)	47 (49)	53 (58)	40 (49)	60	107

BIBLIOGRAPHY

BIBLIOGRAPHY

Albright, W. F., "The Earliest Forms of Hebrew Verse", *JPOS* II (1922), pp. 69-86.

__________, "Some Additional Notes on the Song of Deborah", *JPOS* II (1922), pp. 284-85.

__________, "The Names 'Israel' and 'Judah' with an Excursus on the Etymology of *Tôdâh* and *Tôrâh*", *JBL* XLVI (1927), pp. 168-78.

__________, "The North-Canaanite Poems of *Al'êyân Ba*ᶜ*al*", *JPOS* XIV (1934), pp. 1-40 (renumbered reprint).

__________, "The Song of Deborah in the Light of Archaeology", *BASOR* #62 (1936), pp. 26-31.

__________, "Are the Ephod and the Teraphim Mentioned in the Ugaritic Literature?" *BASOR* #83 (1941), pp. 39-42.

__________, Review of *Introduction to the Old Testament* by Robert H. Pfeiffer, *JBL* LXI (1942), pp. 111-26.

__________, "The Gezer Calendar", *BASOR* #92 (1943), pp. 16-26.

__________, "The Oracles of Balaam", *JBL* LXIII (1944), pp. 207-33.

__________, "The Old Testament and the Canaanite Language and Literature", *CBQ* 7 (1945), pp. 5-31.

__________, *Archaeology and the Religion of Israel*, 2nd ed., Baltimore, 1946.

__________, *From the Stone Age to Christianity*, 2nd ed., Baltimore, 1946.

__________, "The Phoenician Inscriptions of the Tenth Century B.C. from Byblus", *JAOS* 67 (1947), pp. 153-60.

__________, "Exploring in Sinai with the University of California African Expedition", *BASOR* #109 (1948), pp. 5-20.

__________, Editorial Note on the Jerusalem Scrolls, *BASOR* #111 (1948), pp. 2-3.

__________, Review of *L'épithète divine Jahvé Sĕba'ôt: Étude philologique, historique et exégétique* by B. N. Wambacq, *JBL* LXVII (1948), pp. 377-81.

__________, *The Archaeology of Palestine* (Pelican Books, A 199), Harmondsworth, Middlesex, 1949.

Alt, A., "Meros (Jud 5:23)", *ZAW* NS 17 (1940-41), pp. 244-47.

Baentsch, B., *Exodus-Leviticus* (*Handbuch zum Alten Testament*), 1903.

Ball, C. J., "The Blessing of Moses", *Proceedings of the Society of Biblical Archaeology*, XVIII (1896), pp. 118-37.

__________, *The Book of Genesis* (*Sacred Books of the Old Testament*, ed. by P. Haupt), Leipzig, 1896.

Barnes, W. E., *The Peshitta Psalter*, Cambridge, 1904.

__________, *The Psalms with Introduction and Notes*, 2 vols., London, 1931.

__________, "A Taunt-Song in Gen. xlix: 20, 21", *JTS* 33 (1932), pp. 354-59.

Baudissin, W. W. F., *Adonis und Esmun*, Leipzig, 1911.

Beer, G., "Zur Geschichte und Beurteilung des Schöpfungsberichtes Gen 1:1 - 2:4a nebst einem Exkurs über Gen 49:8-12 und 22-26", *Beiträge z. a. w. Karl Budde z. 70. Geburtstag*, ed. by K. Marti, Giessen, 1920 (*BZAW* 34 [1920], pp. 20-30).

__________, *Exodus mit einem Beitrag von K. Galling* (*Handbuch z. A. T.*), Tübingen, 1939.

Bellermann, J. J., *Versuch über die Metrik der Hebräer*, Berlin, 1813.

Bender, A., "Das Lied Exodus 15", *ZAW* 23 (1903), pp. 1-48.

Bertholet, A., *Deuteronomium* (*Kurzer Hand-Commentar z. A. T.*), Leipzig and Tübingen, 1899.

Binns, L. E., *The Book of Exodus*, Cambridge University Press, 1924.

Birnbaum, S. A., "The Date of the Isaiah Scroll", *BASOR* #113 (1949), pp. 33-35.

Böstrom, O. H., *Alternative Readings in the Hebrew of the Books of Samuel*, Rock Island, 1918.

Briggs, C. A., and Briggs, E. G., *A Critical and Exegetical Commentary on The Book of Psalms* (*International Critical Commentary*), 2 vols., New York, 1906.

Brooke, A. E., McLean, N., and Thackeray, H. St. John, (eds.), *The Old Testament in Greek*, Vol. II, Part I (I and II Samuel), Cambridge, 1927.

Brønno, Einar, *Studien über hebräischen Morphologie und Vokalismus*, Leipzig, 1943.

Bruno, A., *Der Rhythmus der altest Dichtung: eine Unters. über die Psalmen I - LXXII*, Leipzig, 1930.

Budde, K., "Das hebräische Klagelied", *ZAW* 2 (1882), pp. 1-52.

__________, *Der Segen Mose's*, Tübingen, 1922.

Burkitt, F. C., "On the Blessing of Moses", *JTS* XXXV (1934), p. 68.

Burney, C. F., *The Book of Judges*, London, 1918.

Burrows, E., *The Oracles of Jacob and Balaam*, London, 1939.

Burrows, M., "Variant Readings in the Isaiah Manuscript", *BASOR* #111 (1948), pp. 16-24.

Buttenwieser, M., *The Psalms*, Chicago, 1938.

Calès, J., *Le Livre des Psaumes*, 2 vols., Paris, 1936.

Caspari, W., *Die Samuelbücher* (*Sellins Kommentar*), Leipzig, 1926.

Cassuto, U., "Il cap. 33 del Deuteronomio e la festa del Capo d'anno nell' antico Israele", *Revista degli Studi Orientali* XI (1928), pp. 233-53.

Causse, A., *Les plus vieux chants de la Bible*, Paris, 1926.

Ceriani, A. M., *Translatio syra pescitto Veteris Testamenti ex codice Ambrosiano, etc.*, 2 vols., Milan, 1876-1883.

Cheyne, T. K., *The Book of Psalms or the Praises of Israel: a new translation with commentary*, 2 vols., London, 1892.

Cobb, W. H., *A Criticism of Systems of Hebrew Metre*, Oxford, 1905.

Cornill, C. H., "Zum Segen Jakobs und zum jawistischer Dekalog", *Studien zur semitischer Philologie und Religionsgeschichte Julius Wellhausen z. 70. Geburtstag*, ed. by K. Marti, Giessen, 1914 (*BZAW* 27), pp. 101-109.

Cross, F. M. Jr., "The Tabernacle: A Study from an Archaeological Point of View", *BA* X (1947), pp. 45-68.

__________, and Freedman, D. N., "A Note on Deuteronomy 33:26", *BASOR* #108 (1947), pp. 6-7.

__________, and __________, "The Blessing of Moses", *JBL* LXVII (1948), pp. 191-210.

__________, and __________, *Early Hebrew Orthography* (*AOS 36*), New Haven: American Oriental Society, 1952.

Cumming, C. G., *Assyrian and Hebrew Hymns of Praise*, New York, 1934.

Delitzsch, F., *Commentar über den Psalter*, 2 vols., Leipzig, 1859-60.

Dillmann, A., *Die Bücher Numeri, Deuteronomium und Josua* (*Kurz. exegetisches Handbuch*), Leipzig, 1886.

Driver, G. R., "Some Hebrew Roots and their Meanings", *JTS* 23 (1922), pp. 69-73.

Driver, S. R., *The Book of Exodus* (*The Cambridge Bible for Schools and Colleges*), Cambridge, 1911.

Driver, S. R., *Notes on the Hebrew Text of the Books of Samuel*, 2nd ed., Oxford, 1913.

__________, *A Critical and Exegetical Commentary on Deuteronomy (ICC)*, New York, 1916.

__________, *The Book of Genesis* (*Westminster Commentaries*), 14th ed. with an appendix by G. R. Driver, London, 1943.

Duhm, B., *Die Psalmen erklärt* (Kurzer H. C. z. A. T.), 2nd ed., Tübingen, 1922.

Dürr, L., "Zum altoriental. Gedankreis 'Der König als Meister im Bogenschiessen, von der Gottheit unterrichtet' (Ps. 18:35; 144:1)", *OLZ* 34 (1931), p. 697.

Eisler, R., "Akkadisch šilu = 'Gebieter' in Gen 49:10", *Mon. Gesch. Wiss. Jud.*, n. f. 33 (1925), pp. 444-46.

__________, "The Babylonian Word 'shilu' (Ruler) in Gen 49:10", *Exp. Times* 36 (1924-25), p. 477.

Eissfeldt, O., "Der Gott des Tabor und seine Verbreitung", *Archiv für Religionswissenschaft* XXXI, pp. 14-41.

Engberg, R., and Albright, W. F., "Historical Analysis of Archaeological Evidence: Megiddo and the Song of Deborah", *BASOR* #78 (1940), pp. 4-9.

Ewald, H., *Die Dichter des Alten Bundes*, 2nd ed., Göttingen, Vol. I, 1866, Vol. II, 1867, Vol. III, 1854 (bound with Vol. II).

Farmer, G., "Jud 5:22", *Exp. Times* 33 (1921-22), p. 93.

Feigin, S. I., "Ḥamor Garim, 'Castrated Ass'", *JNES* V (1946), pp. 230-33.

Fleet, W. F., "Psalm 18:30", *Exp. Times* 42 (1930-31), p. 526.

Friedrich, J., "Zur Einleitungsformel der ältesten phönizischen Inschriften aus Byblos", *Mélanges Dussaud*, Paris, 1939, pp. 37-47.

Gabor, I., *Der hebräische Urrhythmus* (*BZAW* 52), Giessen, 1929.

Garofalo, S., "L'Epinicio d. Mose", *Biblica* 18 (1937), pp. 1-22.

Gaster, T. H., "Deut. 33:12", *Exp. Times* 47 (1935), p. 334.

__________, "Notes on the 'Song of the Sea'", *Exp. Times* 48 (1936-37), p. 45.

__________, "Psalm 29", *JQR* NS, XXXVII (1946), pp. 55-65.

__________, "An Ancient Eulogy on Israel: Deuteronomy 33:3-5, 26-29", *JBL* LXVI (1947), pp. 53-62.

Ginsberg, H. L., "The Rebellion and Death of Ba^{c}lu", *Orientalia* NS V (1936), pp. 161-98.

__________, *Kitvê Ugarît* (Hebrew), Jerusalem, 1936.

__________, "A Ugaritic Parallel to II Sam 1:21", *JBL* LVII (1938), pp. 209-13.

__________, "The North-Canaanite Myth of Anath and Aqhat: II", *BASOR* #98 (1945), pp. 15-23.

__________, *The Legend of King Keret, a Canaanite Epic of the Bronze Age*, *BASOR* Supplementary Series, Nos. 2-3, New Haven, 1946.

__________, "MMŠT and MṢH", *BASOR* #109 (1948), pp. 20-22.

__________, "On Bulletin 108 (Dec. 1947):6-7", *BASOR* #110 (1948), p. 26.

Ginsburg, C. D., *The Old Testament diligently revised according to the Masorah, etc.*, London, 1926.

Glueck, N., "The Theophany of the God of Sinai", *JAOS* 56 (1936), pp. 462-71.

Goodwin, C., "The Meaning of Judg. 5:8b-13", *JBL* LXIII (1944), pp. 259-62.

Gordis, R., "Critical Notes on the Blessing of Moses (Deut. xxxiii)", *JTS* XXXIV, pp. 390-92.

__________, "The Text and Meaning of Deuteronomy 33:27", *JBL* LXVII (1948), pp. 69-72.

Gordon, C. H., *Ugaritic Handbook*, 3 vols., Rome, 1947.

Gressmann, H., *Die Schriften des Alten Testaments*, Göttingen, 1922.

Grether, O., *Das Deboralied. Eine metrische Rekonstruktion*, *Beitr. z. Förderung Christl. Theol.* Band 43, Heft 2, Gütersloh, 1941.

Gunkel, H., *Genesis* (*Handbuch z. A. T.*), Göttingen, 1902.

__________, *Die Psalmen* (Nowack's *H. z. A. T.*), Göttingen, 1926.

Harris, Z. S., *A Grammar of the Phoenician Language*, New Haven, 1936.

Haupt, P., "Moses' Song of Triumph", *AJSL* XX (1903-04), pp. 149-72.

__________, "Die Schlacht von Taanach", *Studien zur semitischen Philologie und Religionsgeschichte* (Julius Wellhausen Festschrift), ed. by K. Marti (*BZAW* 27), 1914, pp. 191-225.

Heinisch, P., *Das Buch Genesis übers. u. erkl.* (*Die Hl. Schrift des A. T.*), Bonn, 1930.

Hitzig, F., *Die Psalmen*, Leipzig and Heidelberg, 1863.

Holzinger, H., *Exodus* (*Kurzer Hand-Commentar z. A. T.*), Tübingen, 1900.

Horst, F., "Einiges zum Text von Gen. 49", *OLZ* 33 (1930), pp. 1-3.

Jacobsen, T., "Primitive Democracy in Ancient Mesopotamia", *JNES* II (1943), pp. 159-72.

Jastrow, M., "Light Thrown on some Biblical Passages by Talmudic Usage", *JBL* 11 (1892), pp. 126-30.

Jirku, A., "Der Juda-Spruch Genesis 49:8ff. und die Texte von Ras Samra", *JPOS* 15 (1935), p. 125.

Joüon, P., "Gen 49:11 סוּת", *Biblica* 21 (1940), p. 58.

Junker, H., *Das Buch Deuteronomium übers. u. erkl.* (*Die Hl. Schrift des A. T.*), Bonn, 1933.

Kahle, P., *Masoreten des Westens*, Stuttgart, 1927.

__________, *The Cairo Geniza* (The Schweich Lectures for 1941), London, 1947.

Kellett, E. E., "Some Old Testament Notes and Queries, Gen. 49:4, 18, 24", *Exp. Times* 33 (1921-22), p. 426.

Kirkpatrick, A. F., *The First and Second Books of Samuel in the R. V., Introduction and Notes* (*The Cambridge Bible*), Cambridge, 1930.

Kittel, R., *Die Psalmen* (*Kommentar z. A. T.*), Leipzig, 1922, 5th ed., 1929.

Knudtzon, J. A. (with Weber, O., and Ebeling, E.), *Die El-Amarna-Tafeln*, Parts I and II, Leipzig, 1915.

König, E., *Das Deuteronomium*, Leipzig, 1917.

__________, *Die Genesis eingeleitet, übers. u. erkl.*, Gütersloh, 1919.

__________, *Die Psalmen eingeleitet, übers. u. erkl.*, Gütersloh, 1927.

Kraft, C. F., *The Strophic Structure of Hebrew Poetry*, Chicago, 1938.

Lagarde, P. de, *Psalterium iuxta Hebraeos Hieronymi*, Leipzig, 1874.

Ley, J., *Die metrischen Formen der hebräischen Poesie*, Leipzig, 1866.

__________, *Gründzüge des Rhythmus, des Vers- und Strophenbaues in der hebräischen Poesie*, Halle, 1875.

__________, *Leitfaden der Metrik der hebräischen Poesie*, Halle, 1887.

Linder, I., "Das Siegeslied des Moses, Ex. 15", *Zts. f. Kath. Theol.* 44 (1920), pp. 43-77.

Lowth, R., *Lectures on the Sacred Poetry of the Hebrews*, trans. by G. Gregory, Andover, 1829.

McNeile, A. H., *The Book of Exodus (Westminster Commentaries)* 2nd ed., London, 1917.

Margoliouth, D. S., "The Fifth Chapter of the Book of Judges", *Expositor*, s. 8, v. 18 (1919), pp. 207-33.

Mendelsohn, I., "State Slavery in Ancient Palestine", *BASOR* #85 (1942), pp. 14-17.

__________, *Slavery in the Ancient Near East*, New York, 1949.

Moore, G. F., *A Critical and Exegetical Commentary on Judges* (*ICC*), New York, 1895.

Morgenstern, J., "The Divine Triad in Biblical Mythology", *JBL* LXIV (1945), pp. 15-37.

Mowinckel, S., *Psalmenstudien (Videnskapsselkapets Skrifter. II Hist.-Filos. Klasse)*
I. *Äwän und die individuellen Klagepsalmen*, 1921, No. 4 (Kristiania, 1921).
II. *Das Thronbesteigungsfest Jahwäs und der Ursprung der Eschatologie*, 1921, No. 6 (Kristiania, 1922).
III. *Kultprophetie und prophetische Psalmen*, 1922, No. 1 (Kristiania, 1923).
IV. *Die technischen Termini in dem Psalmenüberschriften*, 1922, No. 2 (Kristiania, 1923).

Nestle, E., *Psalterium Tetraglottum*, Tübingen, 1879.

__________, "Miscellen", *ZAW* 16 (1896), pp. 321-27.

Nötscher, F., "Gen 49:10 שילה = akk. šēlu", *ZAW* 47 (1929), pp. 323-25.

Noth, M., *Das System der Zwölf Stämme Israels*, Stuttgart, 1930.

Nowack, W., *Richter, Ruth u. Bücher Samuelis* (Handbuch z. A. T.), Göttingen, 1902.

Nyberg, H. S., "Deuteronomium 33:2-3", *ZDMG* 92 (1938), pp. 320ff.

Oesterley, W. O. E., *Ancient Hebrew Poems*, New York, 1938.

__________, *The Psalms*, 2 vols., London, 1940.

Patton, J. H., *Canaanite Parallels in the Book of Psalms*, Baltimore, 1944.

Pedersen, J., *Israel, Its Life and Culture*, 4 vols. in 2, trans. by A. Møller and A. I. Fausbøll, London, 1926-40.

Perles, F., "On the Strophic Form of Exodus 15", *JQR* NS 17 (1926-27), pp. 403-404.

Peters, J. P., "Jacob's Blessing", *JBL* VI (1886), pp. 99-116.

Pfeiffer, R. H., *Introduction to the Old Testament*, New York, 1941; 2nd ed., 1948.

Phythian-Adams, W. J., "On the Date of the 'Blessing of Moses'", *JPOS* III (1923), pp. 158-66.

Piatti, T., "Una nuova interpretazione metrica, testuale, esegetica, del Cantico di Dèbora (Giudici 5:2-31)", *Biblica* 27 (1946), pp. 65-106, 161-209, 434.

Posnanski, A., *Schiloh, ein Beitrag zur Geschichte der Messiaslehre: I. Die Auslegung von Gen 49:10 im Altertume bis zu Ende des Mittelalters*, Leipzig, 1904.

Power, E., "He asked for water, milk she gave (Iud. 5:25)", *Biblica* 9 (1928), p. 47.

Rahlfs, A., *Septuaginta*, 2 vols., Stuttgart, 1935.

Robinson, H. W., "The Council of Yahweh", *JTS* XLIV (1943), pp. 151-57.

de Rossi, G. B., *Variae Lectiones Veteris Testamenti*, Parma, 1785.

Rudolph, W., "Textkritische Anmerkungen zum Richterbuch", *Festschrift Otto Eissfeldt zum 60. Geburtstage 1. September 1947* (ed. by J. Fück), Halle, 1947, pp. 199-212.

Saalshütz, J. L., *Form und Geist der biblisch-hebräischen Poesie*, Königsberg, 1853.

Scheys, H., "Deux notes sur les Psaumes (72:16; 18:11)", *Le Muséon* 43 (1930), pp. 386-88.

Schmidt, H., "Das Meerlied Ex 15:2-19", *ZAW* 49 (1931), NF 8, pp. 59-66.

__________, *Die Psalmen* (*Handbuch z. A. T.*), Tübingen, 1934.

Sellin, E., "Das Deboralied", *Festschrift Otto Procksch*, Leipzig, 1934, pp. 149-66.

__________, "Zu dem Judasspruch im Jaqobssegen Gen 49:8-12 und im Mosesegen Deut 33:7", *ZAW* 60 (1944), pp. 57-67.

Sievers, E., *Metrische Studien. I: Studien zur hebräischen Metrik*, Leipzig, 1901. *II: Die hebräischen Genesis*, Leipzig, 1904.

Skinner, J., *A Critical and Exegetical Commentary on Genesis* (*ICC*), New York, 1910.

Slotki, I. W., "The Song of Deborah", *JTS* 33 (1932), pp. 341-54.

__________, "Longer and Shorter Versions of Ancient Hebrew Poems", *AJSL* 50 (1933), pp. 15-31.

Smith, G. A., *The Early Poetry of Israel in its Physical and Social Origins* (The Schweich Lectures for 1910), London, 1912.

__________, *The Book of Deuteronomy*, 2nd ed., Cambridge, 1919.

Smyth, K., "The Prophecy concerning Juda, Gen 49:8-12", *CBQ* 7 (1945), pp. 290-305.

Snaith, N., "Judges 5:8", *Exp. Times* 41 (1929-30), p. 140.

Sonne, I., "Genesis 49:25-26", *JBL* LXV (1946), pp. 303-06.

Steuernagel, C., *Das Deuteronomium übers. u. erkl.* (*Handkommentar z. A. T.*), 2nd ed., Göttingen, 1923.

Strack, H. L., *Die Bücher Genesis, Exodus, Leviticus und Numeri* (*Kurz. Kom. z. d. Hl. Schriften*), München, 1894.

Sukenik, E. L., מגילות גנוזות (from an ancient genizah which was found in the Wilderness of Judah), *Preliminary Report*, (Hebrew), Jerusalem, 1948.

Sukenik, Y., "Note on t̲l̲t̲ *swsm* in the Legend of Keret", *JCS* II (1948), pp. 11-12.

Thureau-Dangin, F., *Rituels accadiens*, Paris, 1921.

__________, *Textes Cunéiformes* (Louvre). Tome VI *Tablettes d'Uruk*, Paris, 1922.

Trever, J. C., "A Paleographic Study of the Jerusalem Scrolls", *BASOR* #113 (1949), pp. 6-23.

Vercellone, C., *Variae Lectiones Vulgatae Latinae Bibliorum*, II, Rome, 1864.

Von Hoonacker, A., "La bénédiction de Moïse", *Le Muséon* XLII (1929), pp. 42-60.

Wellhausen, J., *Prolegomena zur Geschichte Israels*, 4th ed., Berlin, 1895.

Zimmern, H., "Der Jakobssegen und der Tierkreis", *ZA* VII (1892), pp. 161-72.

Zorell, F., "Davidis de Saul et Ionathan nenia", *Biblica* 2 (1921), pp. 360-63.

__________, "Zu Ps. 18:27", *Biblica* 9 (1928), p. 224.

Addenda

Albright, W. F., "Recent Progress in North-Canaanite Research", *BASOR* #70 (1938), pp. 18-24.

__________, "The Role of the Canaanites in the History of Civilization", *Studies in the History of Culture*, 1942, pp. 11-50.

Baumgartner, W., "Ras Schamra und das Alte Testament", *Theologische Rundschau* NF 12-13 (1940-41).

Bea, A., "Der Zahlenspruch im hebräischen und ugaritischen", *Biblica* 21 (1940), pp. 196-98.

Dussaud, R., "La poésie phénicienne et son rhythme", *Revue de Paris* 44 (1937), pp. 208-16.

Harris, Z. S., "The Structure of Ras Shamra C", *JAOS* 54 (1934), pp. 80-83.

Obermann, J., "How Baal destroyed a Rival", *JAOS* 67 (1947), pp. 195-208.

POSTSCRIPTUM

The original plan of research was simple. In a first study we would examine the inscriptional evidence available from the early periods for the Northwest Semitic languages to determine orthographic practices and patterns, and chart evolutionary developments. Sequence dating and absolute dates would be established by epigraphic analysis of features of the inscriptions other than their orthographic usage.

In a second study we would take the conclusions of the first and apply them to selected biblical texts, to see what could be gained, by rigorous orthographic analysis, in the way of interpretation, elucidation, and clarification of difficult passages, especially in fixed poetic contexts. The earliest Israelite poetry was the immediate target, and the presumption was that embedded in the preserved text of the Hebrew Bible there would be evidence of older orthographic practice surviving despite the scribal revisions in subsequent stages of manuscript transmission, some perhaps as early as the earliest form of Hebrew orthography. This so-called Phoenician spelling of the tenth century B.C. and earlier was marked by strict consonantism in notation, that is, without vowel letters in either the final or medial position. In addition, one of the old poems was preserved in two variant texts, 2 Samuel 22=Psalm 18, and, we hoped, would reflect evidence of both written and oral transmission and perhaps even dialectical differences.

Two dissertations emerged from these studies. Both were completed essentially in the academic year 1947-48 (although the second was not submitted until 1949-50), and served their primary purpose in partially satisfying degree requirements. The first, *Early Hebrew Orthography: The Epigraphic Evidence*, was published in revised form in the American Oriental Series, no. 36, in 1952. In it we set down the basic styles governing spelling practices in the Northwest Semitic inscriptions from the twelfth-eleventh centuries B.C. until the time of the Exile of Judah (early sixth century) and traced the modifications and adaptations of the primary systems of Linear Phoenician after its borrowing into Aramaic and other writing systems, notably

Hebrew. Since its publication, a large number of new inscriptions has turned up, and it has thus been possible to test the major points of the thesis under controlled conditions. The principal affirmations have all been sustained, and only changes in emphasis have been required to accommodate the new data. The main positions, and their modifications, are as follows:

1) All inscriptions using the Linear alphabet are rigorously consonantal in the eleventh-tenth centuries. This includes the Gezer Calendar. Although it has been called "Phoenician," in fact it is signed with the name *'by⌜w⌝*, *'abīyaw*, a good Yahwistic name. In any case, Israel borrowed the classical Phoenician Linear script in the eleventh or early tenth century B.C. Hebrew orthographic practice came under Aramaic influence only in the ninth century at the height of the Aramaic empire which included Israel. The Hebrew alphabet of ca. 800 shows no elements of Aramaic innovation in letter forms, only in orthography.

2) Beginning not later than the ninth century B.C., final vowel letters, *w*, *y*, and *h*, are used systematically in Aramaic. About the same time they are introduced into Moabite, Ammonite, and very likely Hebrew.

3) Beginning no later than the second half of the eighth century B.C., one begins to come upon rare instances of the use of medial vowel letters (*w* = *ū*, *y* = *ī*). This was known to be true of Aramaic at the time the dissertation was written. The evidence for Hebrew suggested that medial vowels were not in use until the second half of the seventh century B.C. The earliest instance of a medial *mater lectionis* in the corpus of Hebrew inscriptions now extant occurs in the Royal Steward Inscription to be dated ca. 700 B.C., so that it appears that the Hebrew pattern is roughly the same as Aramaic. By the early sixth century medial *matres lectionis* are used sporadically, but not yet approaching the frequency exhibited in inscriptions and manuscripts of the Hellenistic and later periods.

With respect to the application of orthographic sequence dating to the biblical text, the results have been less clear. New data, especially from the Qumrân scrolls, and the text-critical resources they provide, suggest unexpected complexity in the orthographic revision and development in the textual families which lie behind the Massoretic text, as well as the imposition of a single orthographic tradition in the Rabbinic recension of the first century of the Christian era. Properly, the era of "Massoretic Fundamentalism" is past particularly in regard to vowel letters and in lesser degree to the consonantal skeletons. The attempt to date a document by survivals of archaic orthographies is a precarious enterprise, and orthographic analysis at best may confirm other typological evidence, linguistic, prosodic, etc. On the other hand, knowledge of the orthographic evolution in Hebrew writing adds an important item to the arsenal of weapons available for attacking recalcitrant texts, including the paleographical development of the Hebrew script, the evolution of Hebrew grammatical usage, and like typological analyses. Archaic orthographies have survived, but most frequently in misunderstood archaic poetry, preserved in disturbed contexts. Thus orthographic analysis offers some help in text-restoration, but as a dating device needs supporting evidence from other sources: variant readings in early Hebrew manuscripts, notably from the texts of the Wilderness of Judah, convincing parallel passages from the Bible or extra-biblical sources, and most important perhaps, variant readings from the Versions. Orthographic study has helped to establish an order or priority in dealing with the text. Thus for the Hebrew Bible, the Massoretic vocalization is latest in time and, while based on "scholarly" intent and practice, is the least reliable of the spelling components as a witness to ancient practice. Next on this scale are the vowel letters, but of these the medial indicators are both later in date and more capricious; they are less important in the determination of lexical and grammatical features. Final vowel letters are older, evolving from a system instituted as early as the ninth century B.C. but undergoing major changes after the contraction of diphthongs. One can differentiate thereby at least two major periods in the usage of final *matres lectionis*. Thus if one reads in the Massoretic text *nʿrw*, "his lad," in an old Samuel manuscript from Qumrân *ʿlmh*, "his lad," the latter is to be judged typologically earlier. *Waw* as a final marker for the 3rd m.s. pronoun replaces *hē* only in post-Exilic times. Finally, with respect to the consonants, one tampers with these--the prime expression of the Phoenician Linear alphabet from its inception--at greatest risk. Orthographic analysis thus provides one more control in text-critical study (including emendation).

Pari passu with the development of orthographic analysis of ancient texts has come vastly increased knowledge of the development of the Hebrew scripts, early Hebrew, its survival in Paleo-Hebrew scripts, and the Jewish scripts, evolving from the Persian chancellery hand (Aramaic) in the course of the Hellenistic age. Knowledge of the sequence of scripts provides a similar approach to problems of corrupt texts and their emendation, and to the primary text-critical task of explaining the origin of variant readings and the selection or reconstruction of superior (or even original) readings. Recovery too of the history of the biblical text in the pre-Rabbinic era has afforded the critic new bases upon which to judge the value and origin of variant texts in Hebrew textual families and later recensions, and in reconstructing the Hebrew text underlying the versions, notably the Old Greek Bible.

Our study of ancient Yahwistic poetry was largely innocent of the new knowledge of Hebrew orthography, paleography, and the textual history of the Bible that emerged after the recovery of the vast cache of manuscripts from Cave 4, Qumrân and later finds in the Wilderness of Judah. The initial draft was written before the publication of the scrolls of Cave 1, Qumrân. Rereading the dissertation, we recognize it to be a period piece, and reissue it as such.

On the basis of the individual studies of the poems in the second dissertation, we had planned to work out a picture of the religion of early Israel--its special character and temper as reflected in the poems, involving words and ideas, the mythopoeic expressions of a way of life grounded equally in historical experience and the confrontation of a divine reality. While the active collaboration of the two authors ended for all practical purposes with the Johns Hopkins theses, our close collegial relationship and mutual scholarly interests have persisted to the present day. Each of us has pursued independently those parts of the unfinished task which are congenial to him, encouraged by the parallel efforts of the other, and constructive criticism freely exchanged. For both the ongoing study of Hebrew poetry has remained a constant, a direct legacy from our teacher W. F. Albright, and through him from his, Paul Haupt.

For Cross this has meant extensive and intensive exploration of the epic and mythic world within which Israel formulated its conceptions and beliefs and the structure of its faith, especially as that world is reflected in Canaanite epic and mythic poetry known chiefly from the texts of Ugarit. Israelite poetic forms and language, and its religious expression, stem in considerable measure from this lively matrix. The analysis of Ugaritic prosody provides thus a background and a control in the analysis of prosodic forms and formulae in earliest Hebrew poetry. Canaanite prosody (reflected in Ugaritic, Phoenician, and Ammonite poetry) provides a first element in a typological sequence from which Isarelite prosody branched off to pursue its own peculiar evolution.

For Freedman the trail of scholarly research has led back to the poems themselves and other examples of the large surviving corpus of poetry in the Bible: to an inductive analysis of their form and structure, their internal organization, and the relationship of the parts. Such studies have led in turn to a reconsideration of the phenomenon of Hebrew poetry and new attempts to describe, analyze, interpret and expound the details of rhythm, meter, strophe, and stanza formation, as well as the many devices and techniques by which the Israelite poet practiced his art. The very fact that biblical poetry belongs to the larger complex of Canaanite and Northwest Semitic verse (as shown conclusively by the continuity between Canaanite and Israelite poetry, including a large common but specialized vocabulary, a common repertoire of oral formulae, and the shared use of other prosodic devices and techniques) shows that Hebrew poetry is the end-product of a long process of development, rather than springing *de novo* from the Wilderness of Sin, or the village culture of the hill-country of Israel and Judah.

The most visible result according to Freedman of a systematic reexamination of methods and systems of metrical counting advocated and used over the decades by scholars of different backgrounds, training, and literary inclination has been the proposal that simple syllable counting is the most effective approach to the question. Instead of isolating stressed syllables to the exclusion of others, or employing a more complicated system for measuring quantity, and then distinguishing long and short syllables, or very long and very short, the provisional conclusion is that these factors either tend to cancel out, especially in lengthy pieces, or cannot be sufficiently discriminated on the basis of present or foreseeable knowledge to justify the efforts required or the results achieved.

Cross has followed a parallel path and finds syllable counting useful in analyzing Canaanite and Hebrew verse. This is not to say that he believes ancient oral poets counted syllables as they composed to music. However, the symmetry in the length of elements in the bicolon or tricolon (but not necessarily in longer sequence of verses) is greater than reflected in stress notation. Until we learn more about Canaanite-Hebrew music, he feels it is best to use a notation which reflects the smallest units into which we can presently divide Canaanite poetry with assurance. There are two basic building blocks in Canaanite and early Hebrew meter: a long colon (l[ongum]) and a short colon (b[reve]) which are combined to form parallelistic verses. These correspond to the stress notation 3 (=l) and 2 (=b). The following metrical patterns are most frequent: l:l and l:l:l, b:b::b:b and l:b::l:b (variants l:b:b:l, b:l:l:b, etc., badly noted in stress analysis as 3:2 or 5:5). Mixed sequences of l:l(:l) and b:b::[b:b(::b:b)] are frequent in early Hebrew lyric poetry.

The move from line (or bicolon) to stanza or other determinable larger units is fraught with danger, and many scholars have denied the presence of regular stanzas in biblical poetry, or at least have challenged the claim that such structures have been identified with any consistency. While progress has been slow and uncertain, that opinion was too negative. According to Freedman, careful investigation has shown that the Hebrew poet used many devices, including refrains, partial refrains, the repetition of key words to signify inclusions, envelope constructions, and frames of different kinds; we are on the threshhold of more impressive discoveries concerning the nature of this genre of literature.

While the original task remains unfinished, and in some sense it is barely started, the study of the early poetry has proved fruitful far beyond the limits of the initial inquiry. The reconstruction of early Israelite religion, whether of the Fathers or of Moses and his followers, requires equal attention to backgrounds: cultural, linguistic, mythological, and historical. The quest has led in all these directions through the ancient Near East, with extensive work by us and our fellow heirs of the Johns Hopkins tradition, our students, and our critics.

Latterly, attention has focussed on historical reconstruction, and both Cross and Freedman have contributed to the elucidation of the complex movements of peoples and the changes in socio-political patterns during the period reflected in the early poems of Israel.

The poetry of early Israel offers a continuing and irresistible challenge to the scholarly community. By reissuing this doctoral dissertation, we happily invite a new as well as an older generation of colleagues to join in the pursuit of common goals.

Frank Moore Cross
David Noel Freedman

August 10, 1975

RECENT BIBLIOGRAPHY

For Hebrew poetry, and specifically the early poems, consult the annotated bibliography at the end of Freedman's "Prolegomenon" to G. B. Gray's *Forms of Hebrew Poetry* (New York: Ktav Publishing House, 1972 [reissue]), pp. xlvii-liii.

In addition, the following articles by Freedman may be listed:

1. On orthography:

"The Massoretic Text and the Qumran Scrolls: A Study in Orthography," *Textus* II (1962) pp. 87-102. To be reprinted in *Qumran and the History of the Biblical Text*, ed. F. M. Cross and Shemaryahu Talmon (Cambridge: Harvard University Press, 1975).

"Orthographic Peculiarities in the Book of Job," *Eretz Israel* 9 (1969) (Albright *Festschrift*) pp. 35-44.

"The Orthography of the Arad Ostraca," *IEJ* 19 (1969), pp. 52-56.

2. On early poetry:

"Some Observations on Early Hebrew" (with F. M. Cross), *Biblica* 53 (1972) pp. 413-20.

"Divine Names and Titles in Early Hebrew Poetry," *Magnalia Dei* (G. E. Wright *Festschrift*), ed. F. M. Cross, Patrick Miller, and Werner Lemke (in press).

"Early Israelite History in the Light of Early Israelite Poetry," *Unity and Diversity: Studies in the Ancient Near East* (Baltimore: Johns Hopkins Press, 1975), pp. 3-35.

"Early Israelite Poetry and Historical Reconstructions," Jerusalem Symposium Volume, ed. F. M. Cross (forthcoming).

"Strophe and Meter in the Song of the Sea," *A Light Unto My Path: Old Testament Studies in Honor of J. M. Myers*, ed. H. N. Bream, R. D. Helm, C. A. Moore (1974), pp. 163-203.

"Psalm 29: A Structural Analysis" (with Franke-Hyland), *HTR* 66 (1973) pp. 237-56.

"The Refrain in David's Lament Over Saul and Jonathan," *Ex Orbe Religionum. Studia Geo Widengren*, ed. J. Bergman, K. Drynjeff, H. Ringgren (Studies in the History of Religions, Vol. XII [1972]), pp. 115-126.

3. On other poetry:

"Prolegomenon" to Gray's *Forms of Hebrew Poetry* (see above).

"The Structure of Psalm 137," *Near Eastern Studies in Honor of William Foxwell Albright*, ed. H. Goedicke (Baltimore: Johns Hopkins Press, 1971), pp. 187-205.

"Psalm 23," George Cameron *Festschrift* (in press).

"Acrostics and Metrics," *HTR* 65 (1972), pp. 367-392.

"The Structure of Job 3," *Biblica* 49 (1968), pp. 503-508.

"The Aaronic Benediction," John L. McKenzie *Festschrift* (in press).

The following articles and studies by Cross may be listed:

1. On orthography:

"The Oldest Manuscripts from Qumran," *JBL* 74 (1955), pp. 147-172.

"The Contribution of the Discoveries at Qumran to the Study of the Biblical Text," *IEJ* 16 (1966), pp. 81-95.

2. On early poetry:

"The Divine Warrior in Israel's Early Cult," *Studies and Texts III: Biblical Motifs*, ed. A. Altmann (Cambridge: Harvard University Press, 1966), pp. 11-30.

"The Song of the Sea and Canaanite Myth," *Journal for Theology and the Church* 5 (1968), pp. 1-25.

"Phoenician Incantations on a Plaque of the Seventh Century B.C. from Arslan Tash in Upper Syria" (with R. J. Saley), *BASOR* 197 (1970), pp. 42-49.

"Prose and Poetry in the Mythic and Epic Texts from Ugarit," *HTR* 67 (1974), pp. 1-15.

"Note on the Ammonite Inscription from Tell Sīrān," *BASOR* 212 (1973), pp. 12-15.

"Leaves from an Epigraphist's Notebook" (esp. "A Second Incantation from Arslan Tash"), *CBQ* 36:4 (October, 1974), pp. 486-494.

A number of early Hebrew poems are analyzed and discussed in *Canaanite Myth and Hebrew Epic* (Cambridge: Harvard University Press, 1973). The following guide may be useful:

"The Song of the Sea," Exodus 15, pp. 121-144.

"The Blessing of Moses," Deuteronomy 33:2-3, 26-29, pp. 101, 157.

"The Song of Deborah," Judges 5:4f., 8, pp. 100, 122.

"The Lament of David," I Samuel 1:19-28, pp. 122f.

2 Samuel 22 = Ps. 18:8-16, pp. 158f.

"The Last Words of David," 2 Samuel 23:1-5, pp. 234-37.

"The Song of Habakkuk," Hab. 3:3-6, pp. 102f., 140.

Psalm 24:7-14, pp. 91-99.

Psalm 29, pp. 151-56.

Psalm 68:18, p. 102.

Psalm 77:17-20, p. 136.

Psalm 89:20-37, pp. 258-60.

Psalm 97:1-6, p. 162.

Psalm 114, pp. 138-40.

Psalm 132, pp. 94-97, 232-34.

Attention may also be called to Harvard dissertations dealing with Ugaritic and Hebrew poetry, including those of Douglas Stuart, "Studies in Early Hebrew Meter" (to be published in Harvard Semitic Monographs); Arlis John Ehlen, "The Poetic Structure of a Hodayah from Qumran: An Analysis of Grammatical, Semantic, and Auditory Correspondence in 1QH 3:19-36" (a programmatic essay on late Hebrew poetry); and Stephen Geller (a study of Ugaritic and early Hebrew poetry from the point of view of new linguistic approaches to poetics, to be completed in 1975).